HAL LEONARD COUNTRY GUITAR SONGS

SECOND EDITION

GUITAR METHOD
Supplement to Any Guitar Method

Standard Notation and Tablature for 10 Complete Songs by Artists
Including Chris Stapleton, Eric Church, and Johnny Cash

AUDIO ACCESS INCLUDED

PLAYBACK+
Speed • Pitch • Balance • Loop

To access audio visit:
www.halleonard.com/mylibrary

"Enter Code"
3691-3938-5044-2677

ISBN 978-1-70510-884-0

HAL•LEONARD®

Visit Hal Leonard Online at
www.halleonard.com

Contact us:
Hal Leonard
7777 West Bluemound Road
Milwaukee, WI 53213
Email: info@halleonard.com

In Europe, contact:
Hal Leonard Europe Limited
42 Wigmore Street
Marylebone, London, W1U 2RN
Email: info@halleonardeurope.com

In Australia, contact:
Hal Leonard Australia Pty. Ltd.
4 Lentara Court
Cheltenham, Victoria, 3192 Australia
Email: info@halleonard.com.au

Amie

Words and Music by Craig Fuller

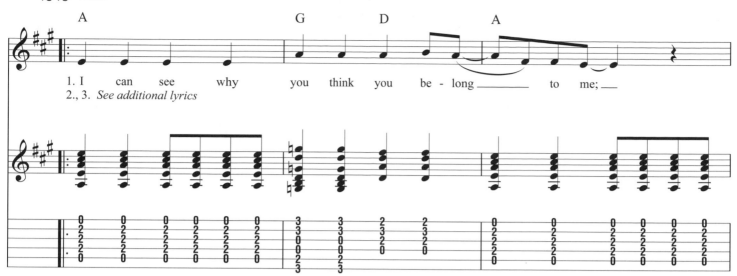

1. I can see why you think you be-long _____ to me; _____
2., 3. *See additional lyrics*

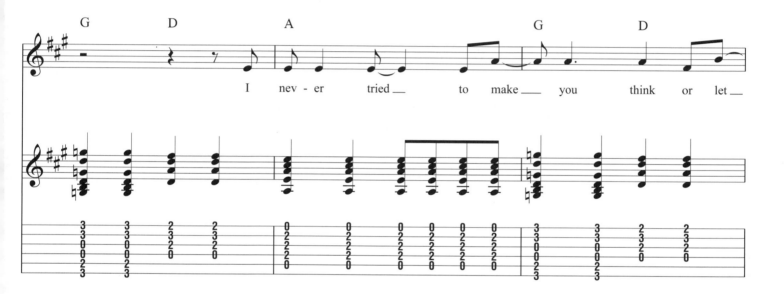

I nev-er tried ___ to make ___ you think or let ___

___ you see one _____ thing for ___ your-self. _____

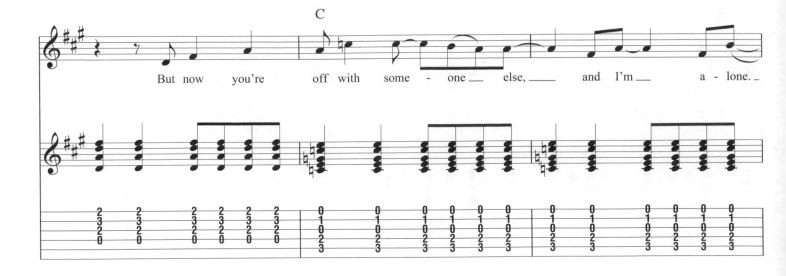

But now you're off with some - one _ else, _ and I'm _ a - lone. _

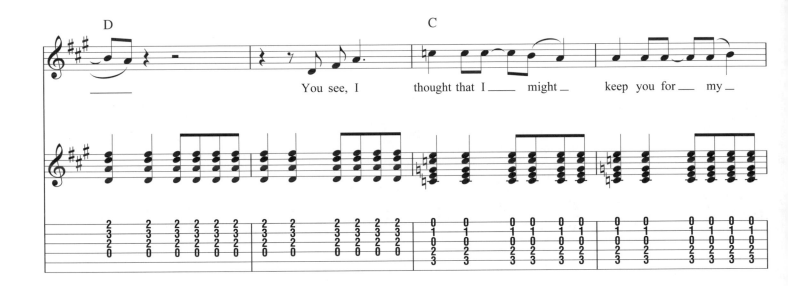

_ You see, I thought that I _ might _ keep you for _ my _

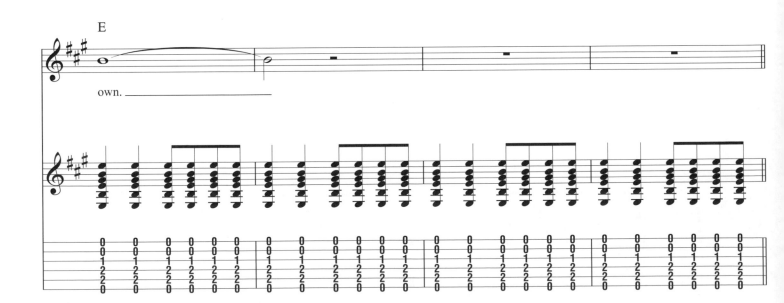

own. _

3rd time, substitute Fill 1

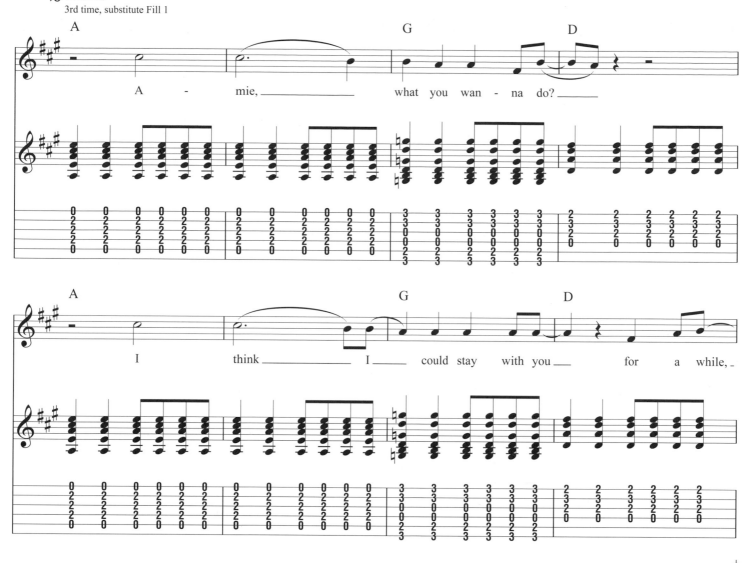

A - mie, _____ what you wan - na do? _____

I _____ think _____ I _____ could stay with you _____ for a while, _

To Coda 2

____ may - be long - er if I ____ do. _____

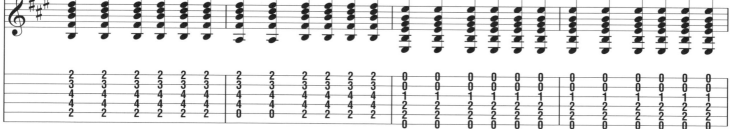

Fill 1

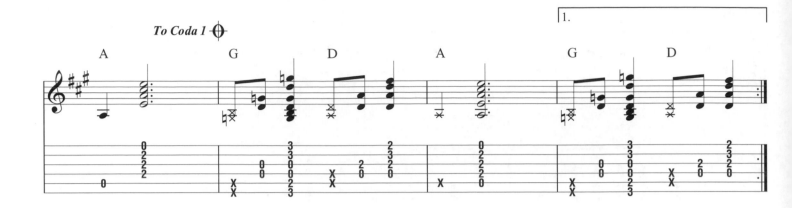

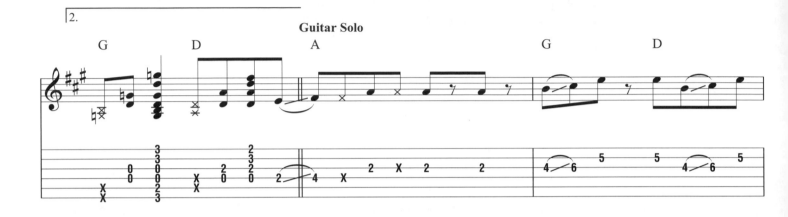

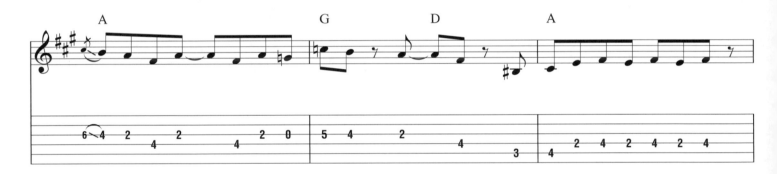

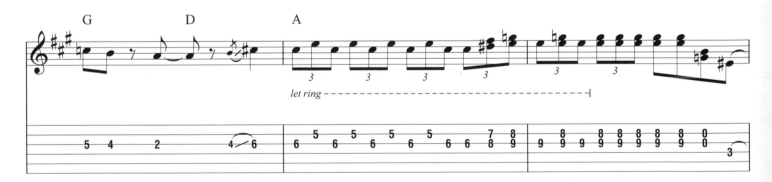

D.S. al Coda 1

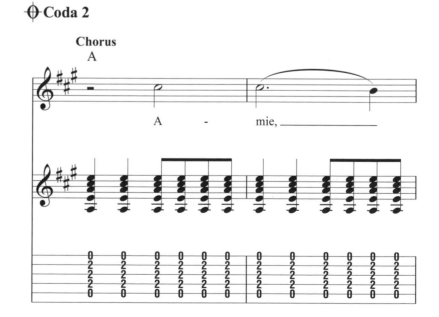

⊕ Coda 1

D.S.S. al Coda 2

⊕ Coda 2

Chorus

A - mie,_____

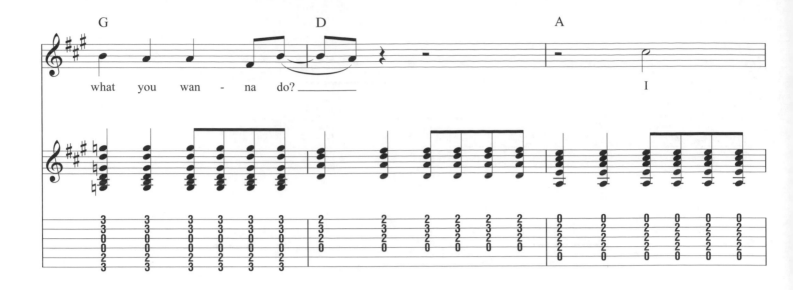

what you wan - na do? _____ I

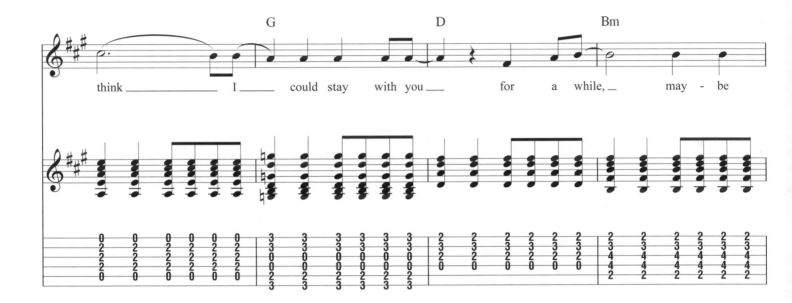

think _____ I _____ could stay with you _____ for a while, _____ may - be

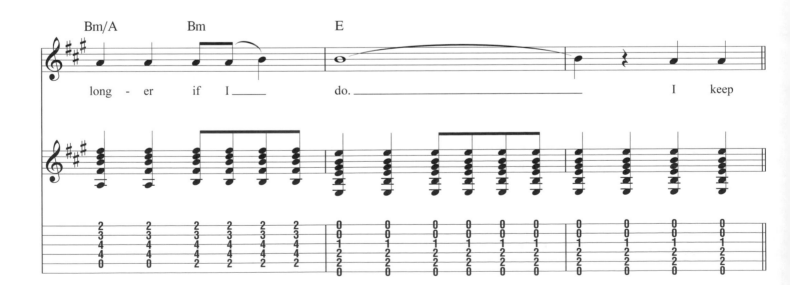

long - er if I _____ do. _____ I keep

Outro

Half-time feel

fall - in' in and out _____ of love _____ with you, _____

let chords ring throughout

don't know what I'm gon - na do. _____

_____ I keep fall - in' in and out _____ of love _____

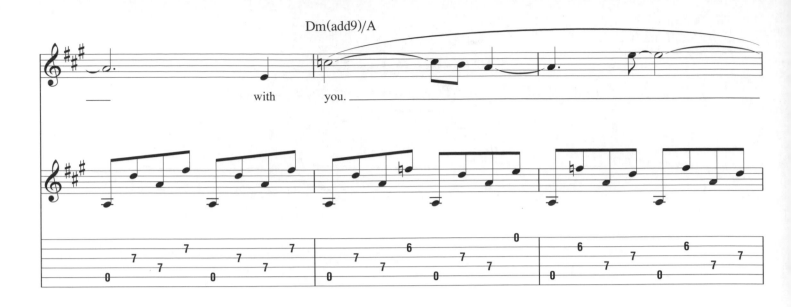

Additional Lyrics

2. Don't you think the time is right for us to find,
   All the things we thought weren't proper
   Could be right in time and can you see
   Which way we should turn together or alone?
   I can never see what's right or what is wrong.
   Would it take too long to see?

3. Now it's come to what you want, you've had your way.
   And all the things you thought before
   Just faded into gray and can you see
   That I don't know if it's you or if it's me?
   If it's one of us I'm sure we both will see.
   Won't ya look at me and tell me...

Country Girl
(Shake It for Me)

Words and Music by Luke Bryan and Dallas Davidson

Intro
Moderate Country ♩ = 106

got a lit-tle boom in my ___ big truck. ___ Gon-na o-pen up the doors and turn ___ it up. ___ Gon-na

stomp my boots in the Geor-gia mud. ___ Gon-na watch you make me fall in love. Get up

on the hood ___ of my dad-dy's trac-tor. Up on the tool - box, it don't mat - ter. Down ___

Pre-Chorus

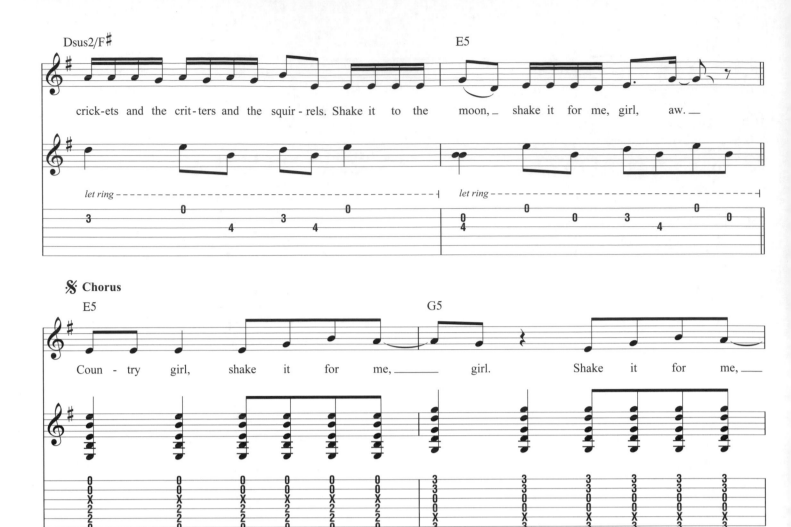

Chorus

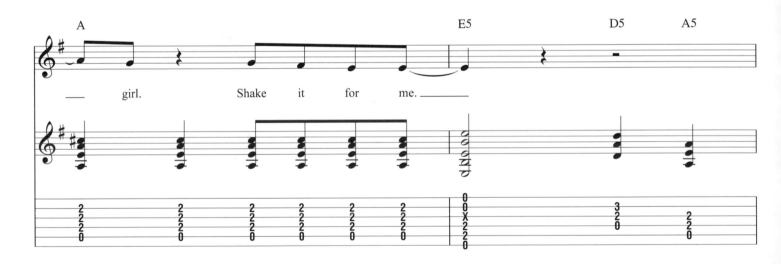

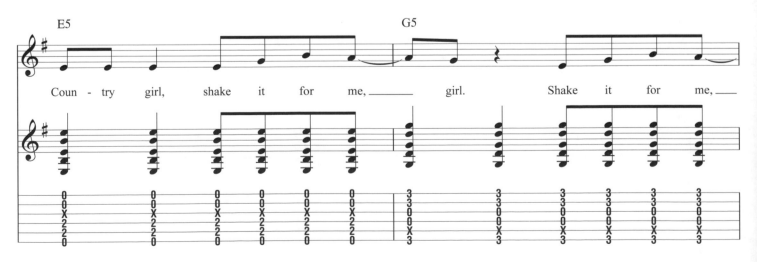

Verse

birds, _ shake it for the bees. _ Shake it for the cat - fish swim - min' down deep in the creek. _ For the

D.S. al Coda 1

crick - ets and the crit - ters and the squir - rels. Shake it to the moon, _ shake it for me, girl.

Coda 1

Guitar Solo

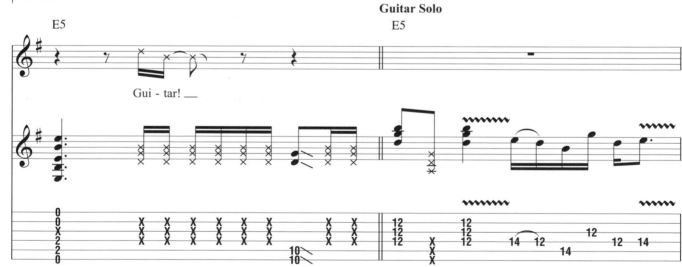

Gui - tar! _

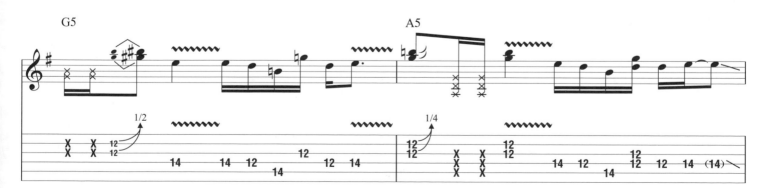

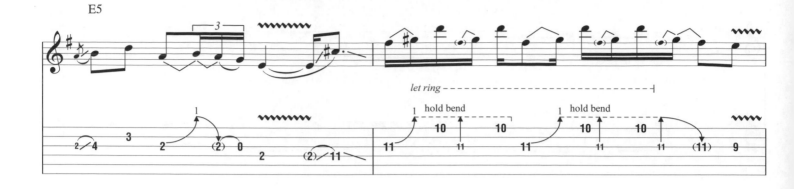

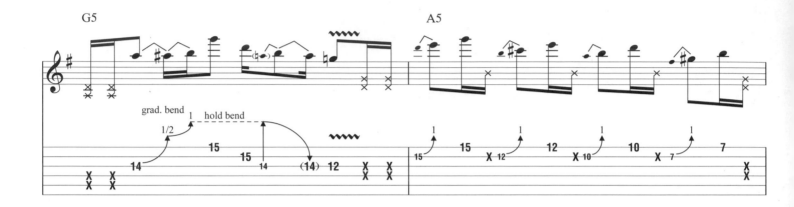

Bridge

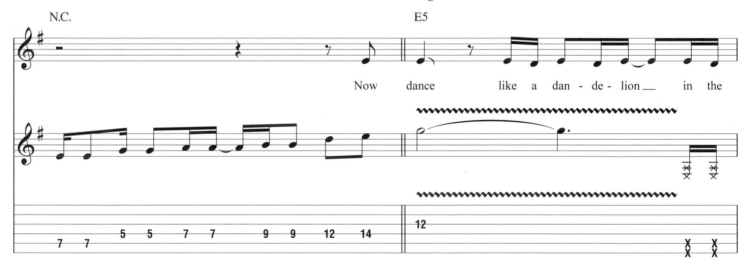

Now dance like a dan-de-lion ___ in the

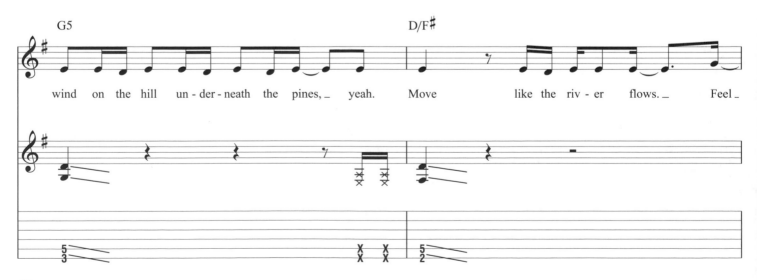

wind on the hill un-der-neath the pines, ___ yeah. Move like the riv-er flows. ___ Feel ___

the kick drum down deep in your toes. ___ All I wan-na do is get to hold - in' you ___ and get to

let ring -

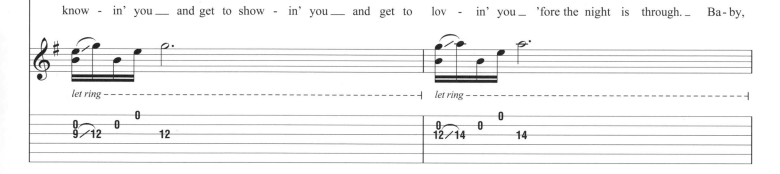

know - in' you ___ and get to show - in' you ___ and get to lov - in' you ___ 'fore the night is through. ___ Ba - by,

let ring - *let ring* -

Pre-Chorus

you know what to do. ___ Shake it for the young bucks sit - tin' in the hon - ky - tonks, ___ for the

let ring -

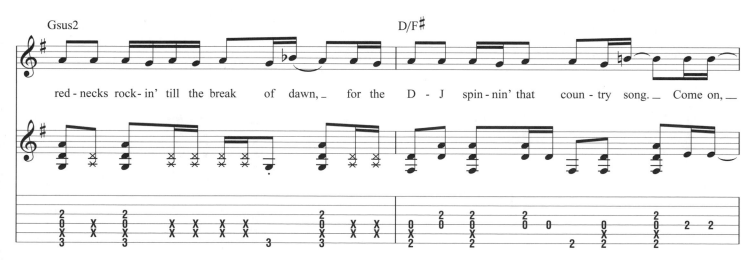

red - necks rock - in' till the break of dawn, ___ for the D - J spin - nin' that coun - try song. ___ Come on, ___

come on, _ come on. _ Shake it for the birds, _ shake it for the bees. _ Shake it for the

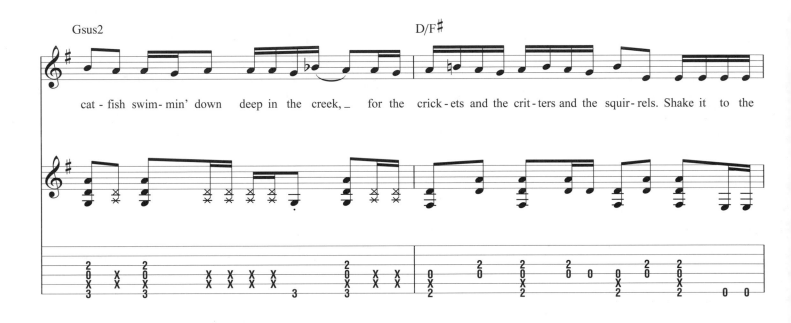

cat-fish swim-min' down deep in the creek, _ for the crick-ets and the crit-ters and the squir-rels. Shake it to the

D.S. al Coda 2

 Coda 2

moon, _ shake it for me, girl, aw.

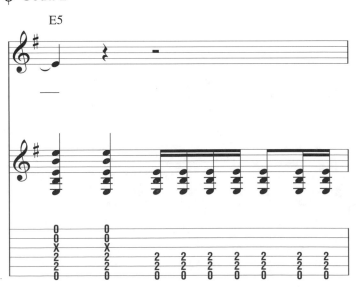

Coun-try girl, — shake it for me, — girl. — Shake it for me, — girl. — Shake it for me. —

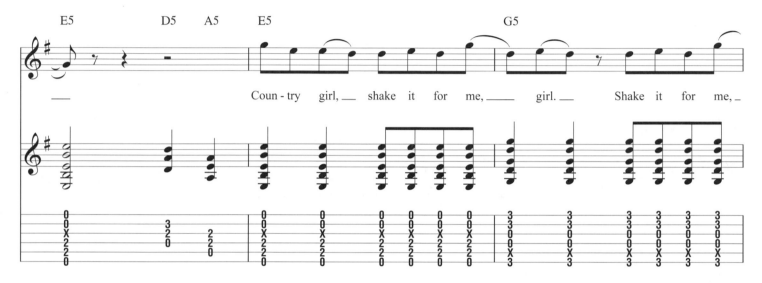

— Coun-try girl, — shake it for me, — girl. — Shake it for me, —

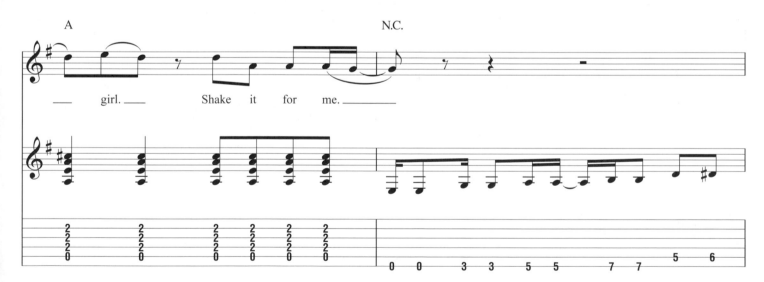

— girl. — Shake it for me. —

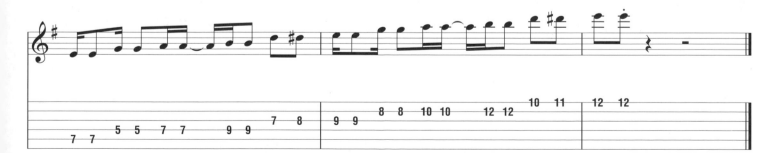

Boot Scootin' Boogie

Words and Music by Ronnie Dunn

down. ___ They got whis - key, wom - en, ___

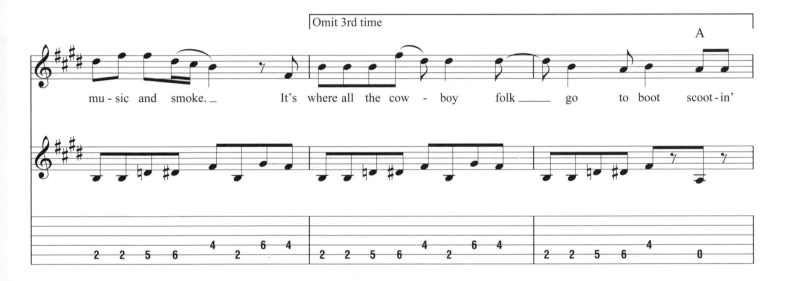

Omit 3rd time

A

mu - sic and smoke. ___ It's where all the cow - boy folk ___ go to boot scoot - in'

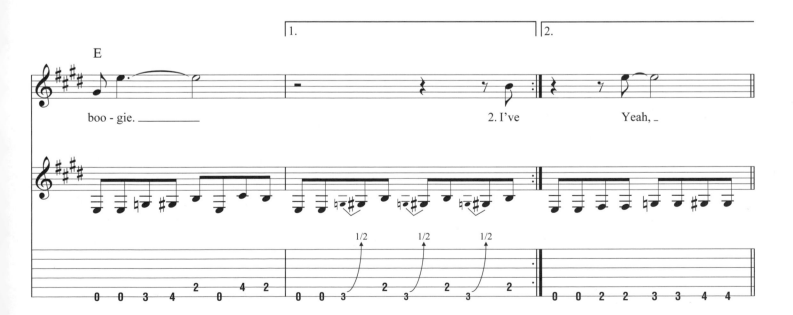

E

1.

2.

boo - gie. _____ 2. I've Yeah, ___

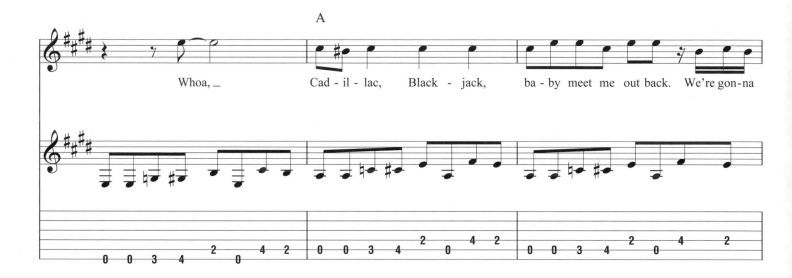

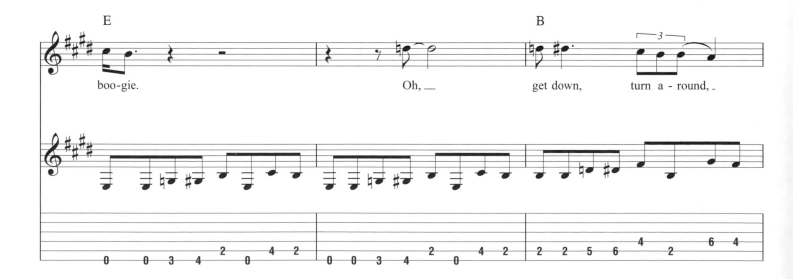

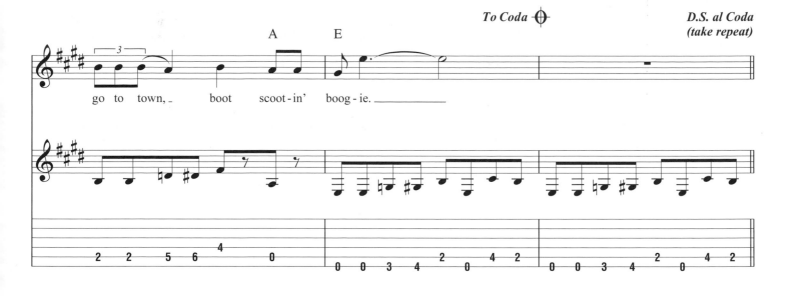

go to town, _ boot scoot-in' boog-ie. _____

✛ **Coda**

Chorus

Whoa, _ heel to toe, do-sa do, come on ba-by, let's go

boot scoot-in'! Yeah, _ Cad-il-lac, Black-jack,

Additional Lyrics

2. I've got a good job, I work hard for my money.
   When it's quittin' time, I hit the door runnin'.
   I fire up my pickup truck and let the horses run.
   I go flyin' down that highway to that hideaway,
   Stuck out in the woods, to do the boot scootin' boogie.

4. The bartender asks me, says, "Son, what will it be?"
   I want a shot at that red-head yonder lookin' at me.
   The dance floor's hoppin' and it's hotter than the Fourth of July.
   I see outlaws, in laws, crooks and straights,
   All makin' it shake doin' the boot scootin' boogie.

Cruise

Words and Music by Chase Rice, Tyler Hubbard, Brian Kelley, Joey Moi and Jesse Rice

*Chord symbols in parentheses represent chord names respective to capoed guitar.
Symbols above reflect actual sounding chords. Capoed fret is "0" in tab.

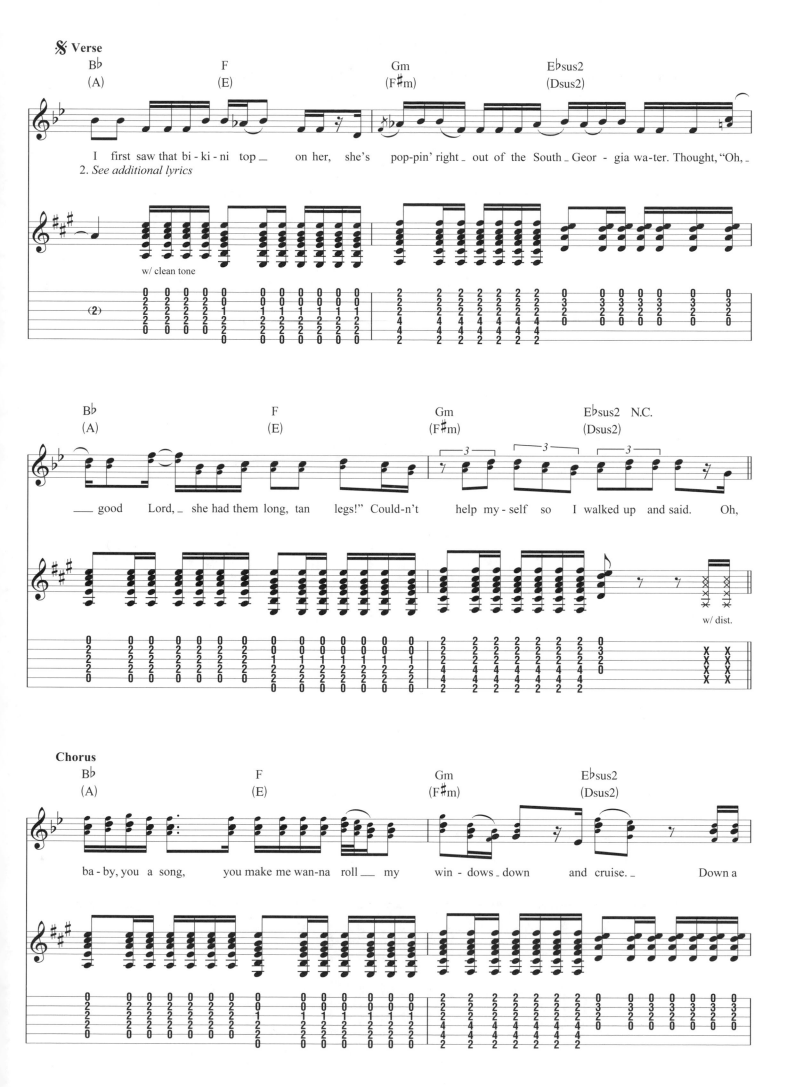

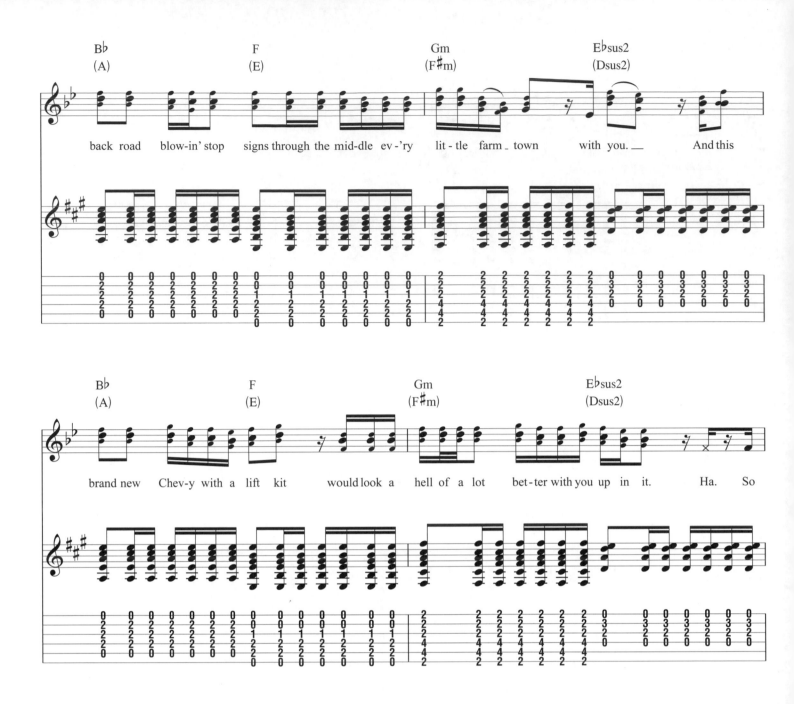

back road blow-in' stop signs through the mid-dle ev-'ry lit-tle farm town with you. ___ And this

brand new Chev-y with a lift kit would look a hell of a lot bet-ter with you up in it. Ha. So

To Coda ⊕

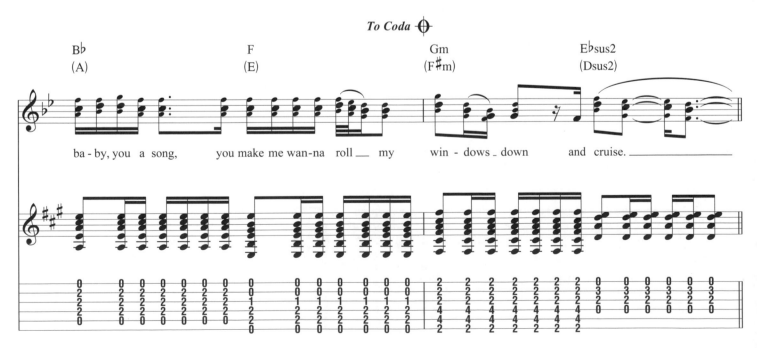

ba-by, you a song, you make me wan-na roll ___ my win - dows _ down and cruise. _____

Interlude

2. Well, she was

Coda

Guitar Solo

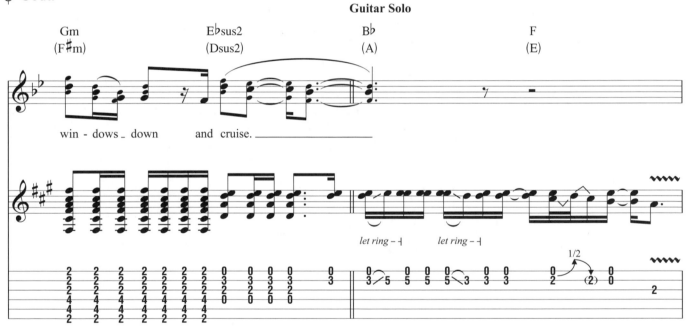

win - dows_ down   and   cruise._____

let ring ⌐   *let ring* ⌐

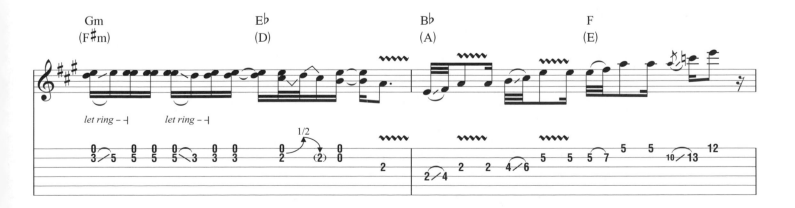

let ring ⌐   *let ring* ⌐

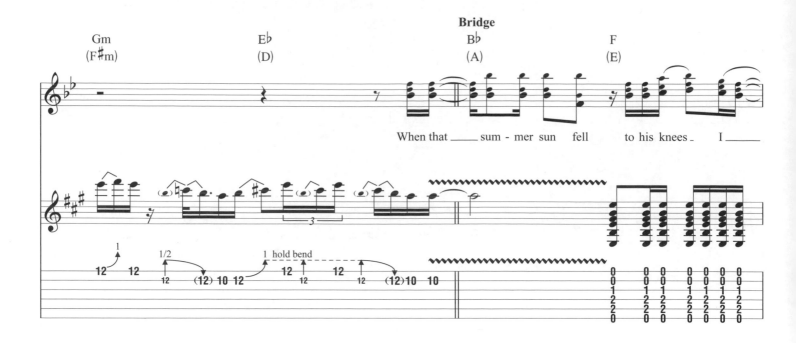

When that ___ sum-mer sun fell to his knees ___ I ___

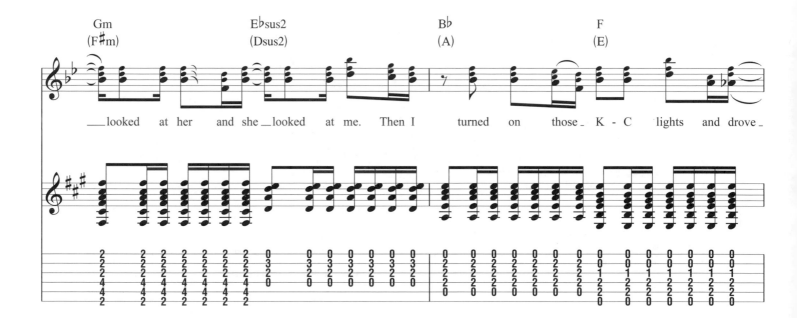

___looked at her and she ___looked at me. Then I turned on those ___ K - C lights and drove ___

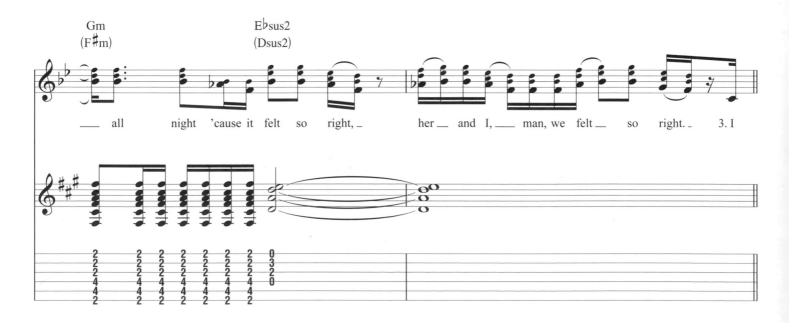

___ all night 'cause it felt so right, ___ her ___ and I, ___ man, we felt ___ so right. ___ 3. I

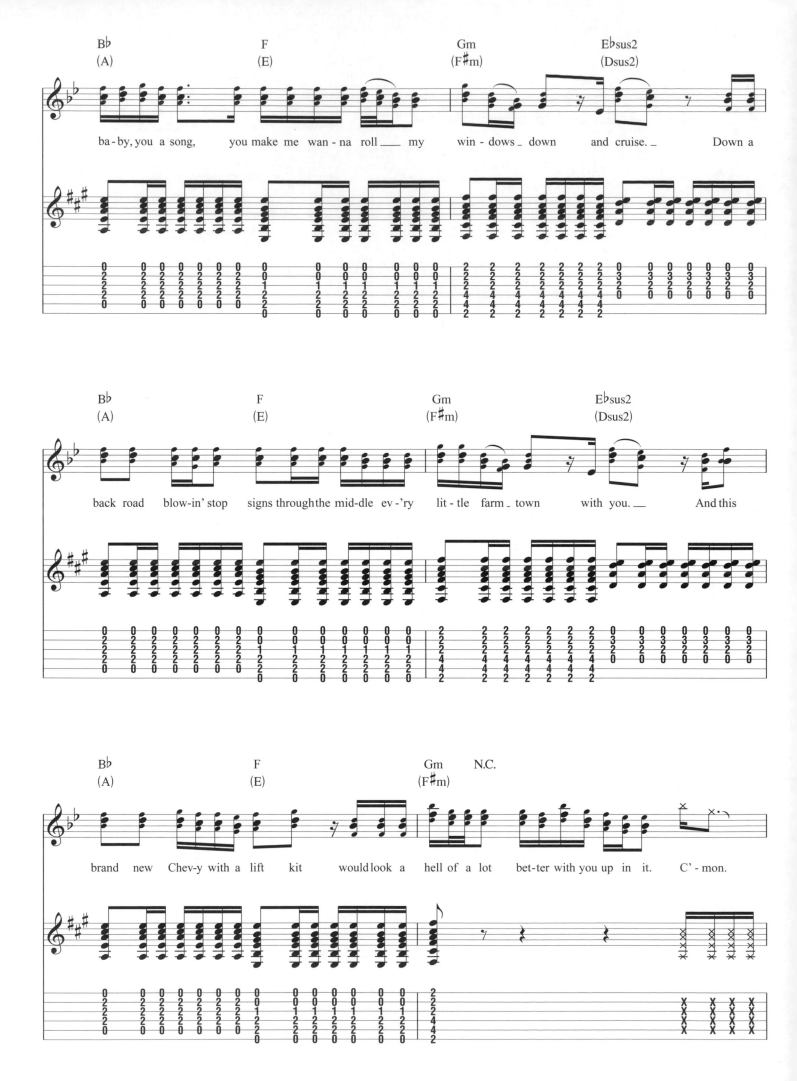

Additional Lyrics

2. Well, she was sippin' on Southern and singin' Marshall Tucker.
   We were fallin' in love in the sweetheart of summer.
   She hopped right up into the cab of my truck and said,
   "Fire it up, let's go get this thing stuck."

Drink in My Hand

Words and Music by Eric Church, Michael Heeney and Luke Laird

Capo III

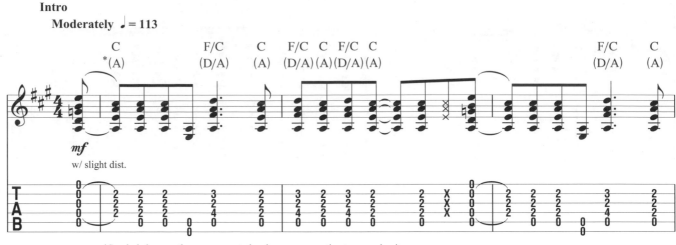

*Symbols in parentheses represent chord names respective to capoed guitar.
Symbols above reflect actual sounding chords. Capoed fret is "0" in tab.

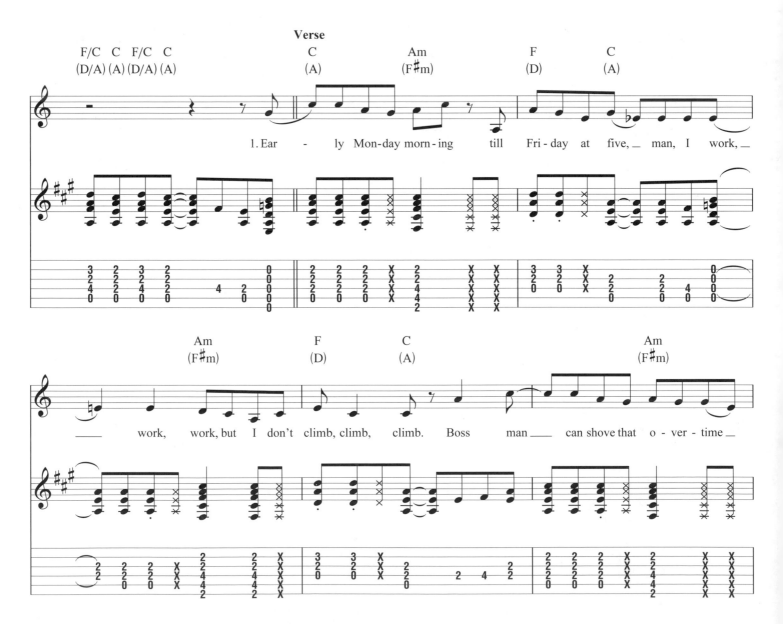

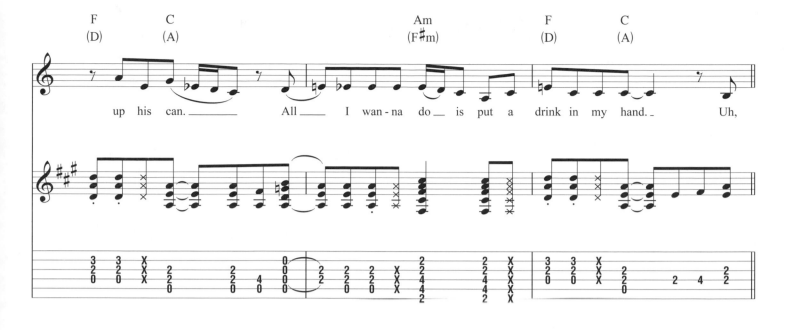

Chorus

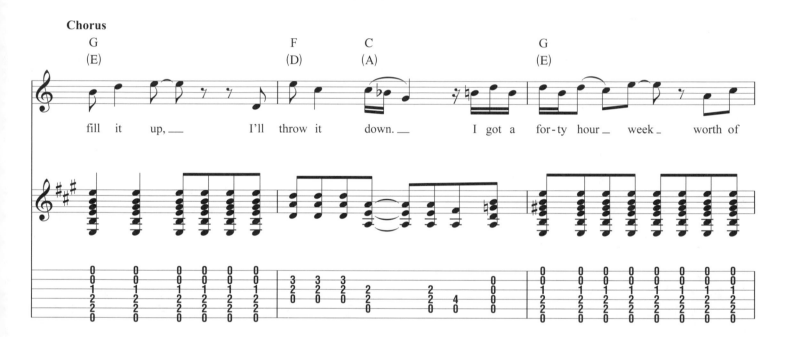

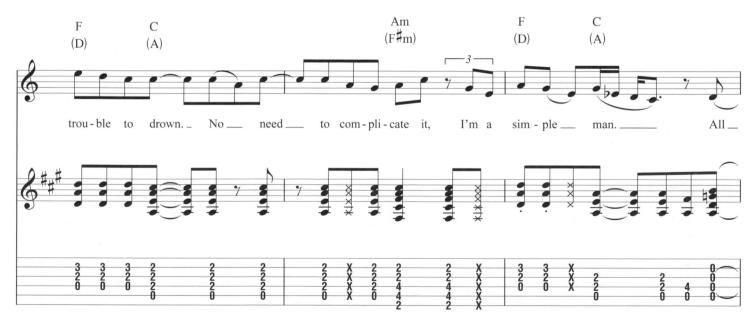

you got - ta do __ is put a drink in my hand. __

Interlude

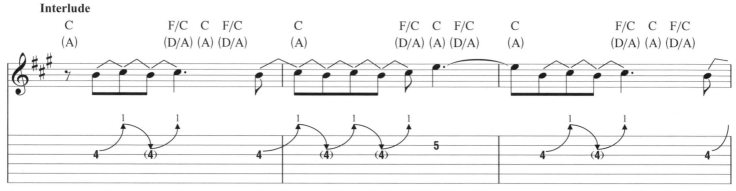

Verse

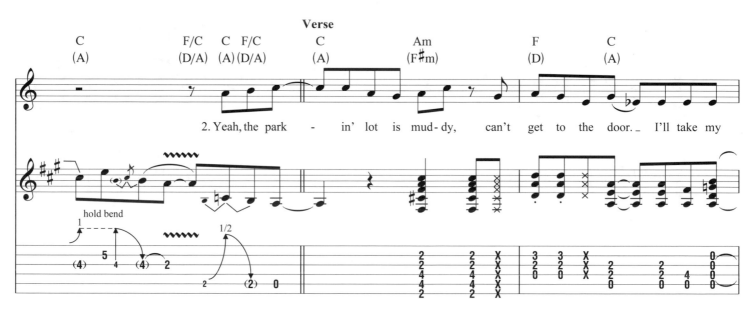

2. Yeah, the park - in' lot is mud - dy, can't get to the door. __ I'll take my

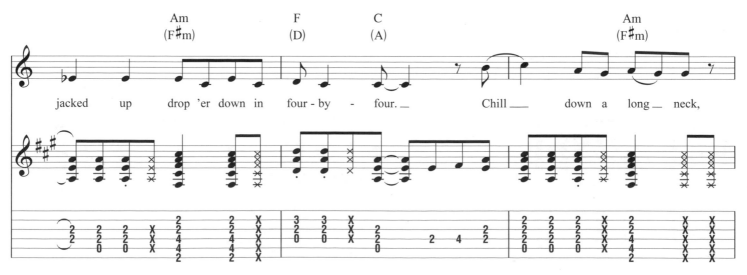

jacked up drop 'er down in four - by - four. __ Chill __ down a long __ neck,

39

Guitar Solo

Make me wan-na go, ___

Bridge

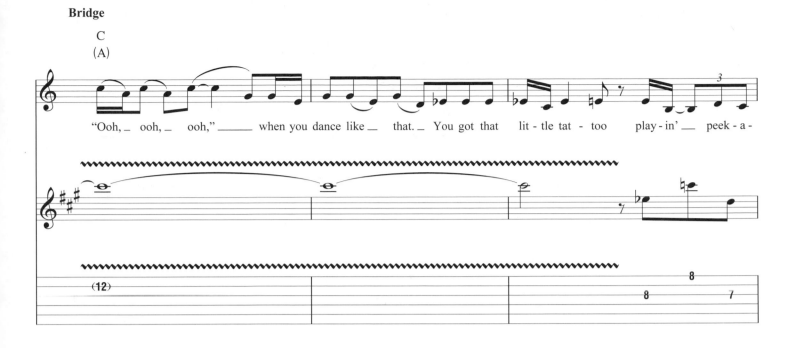

"Ooh,__ ooh,__ ooh,"___ when you dance like__ that.__ You got that lit-tle tat-too play-in'__ peek-a-

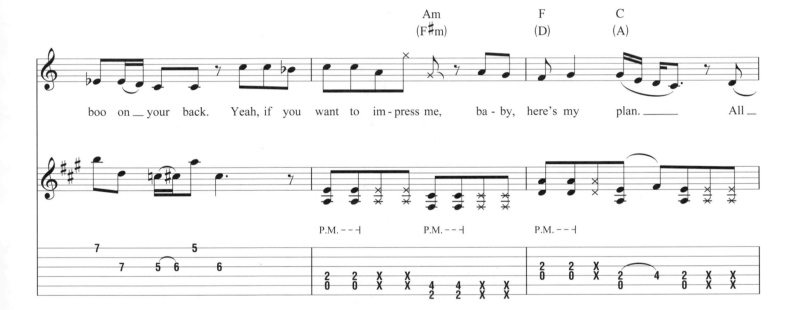

boo on__ your back. Yeah, if you want to im-press me, ba-by, here's my plan.____ All__

D.S. al Coda 1

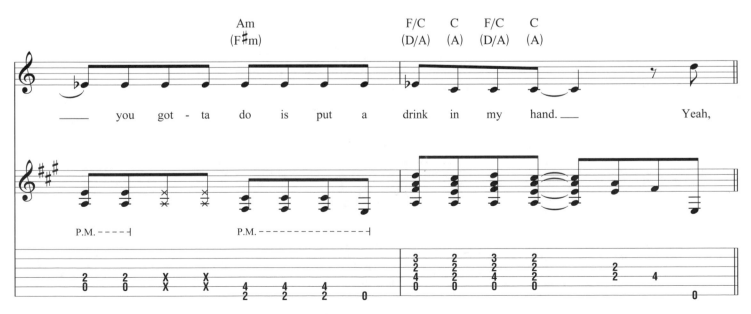

____ you got-ta do is put a drink in my hand.__ Yeah,

⊕ Coda 1

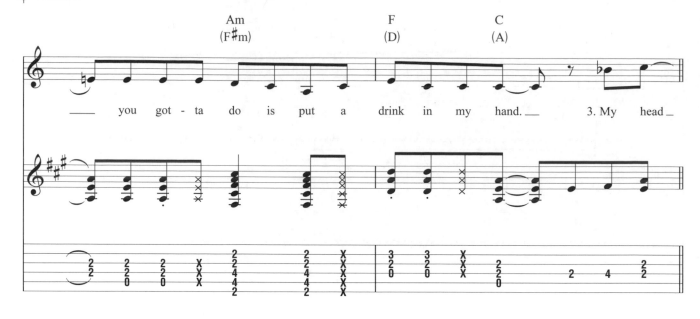

you got-ta do is put a drink in my hand. ___ 3. My head ___

Verse

___ Mon-day morn-in' that a-larm clock sings, ___ it goes bang, bang, bang ___ while it

ring, ring, rings. ___ Yeah, I'm read-y to roll ___ if you wan-na rock a-gain. _____ All ___

42

you got-ta do is put a drink in my hand. ___ Yeah,

Coda 2

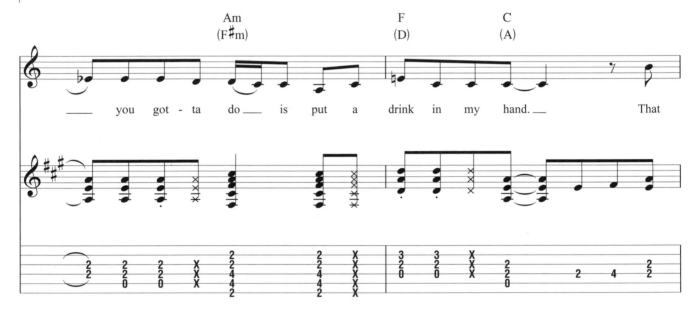

you got-ta do ___ is put a drink in my hand. ___ That

hair of the dog ___ is howl - in', "Hey there, ___ man." ___ All ___

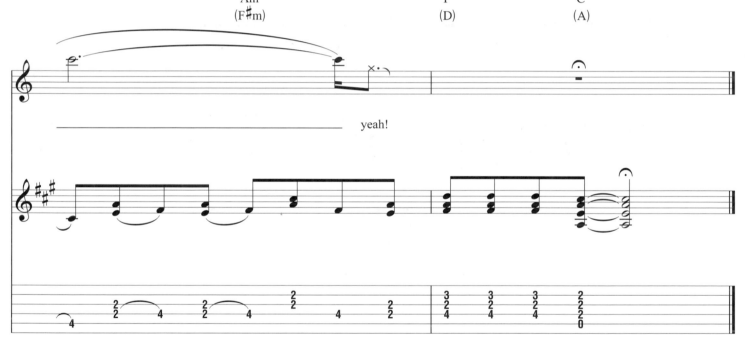

Additional Lyrics

Chorus 2. Yeah, fill it up, I'll throw it down.
When you drive me home, take the long way around.
You'll be my Lois Lane, I'll be your Superman.
All you gotta do is put a drink in my hand. That's-a right!

Chorus 3. Yeah, fill it up, I'll throw it down.
I got a little hung over, still hangin' around.
Yeah, that hair of the dog is howlin', "Hey there, man."
All you gotta do is put a drink in my hand.

Friends in Low Places

Words and Music by DeWayne Blackwell and Earl Bud Lee

Capo II

Intro
Moderately ♩ = 108

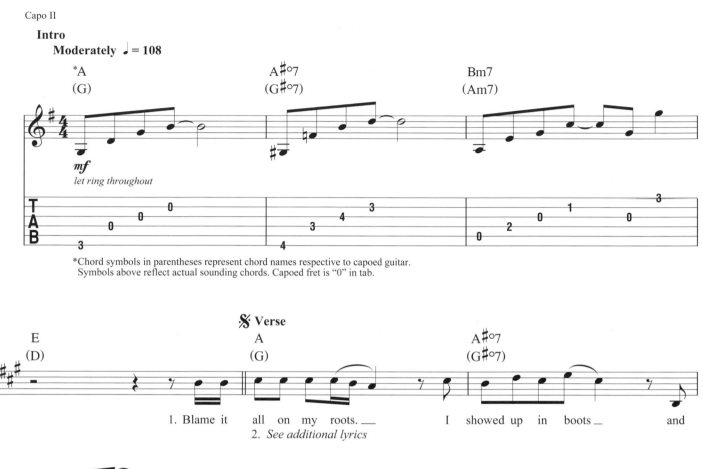

*Chord symbols in parentheses represent chord names respective to capoed guitar.
Symbols above reflect actual sounding chords. Capoed fret is "0" in tab.

𝄋 **Verse**

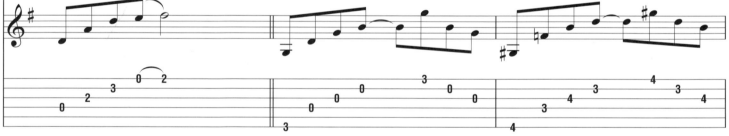

1. Blame it all on my roots. ___ I showed up in boots ___ and
2. *See additional lyrics*

ru - ined your black ___ tie af - fair. ___ The last one to know, ___ the

last one to show, __ I was the last __ one you thought you'd see there. __ And I

saw the sur-prise __ and the fear in his eyes __ when I took his glass __ of cham-pagne, __

and I toast-ed you, __ said, "Hon-ey, we may be through, __ but

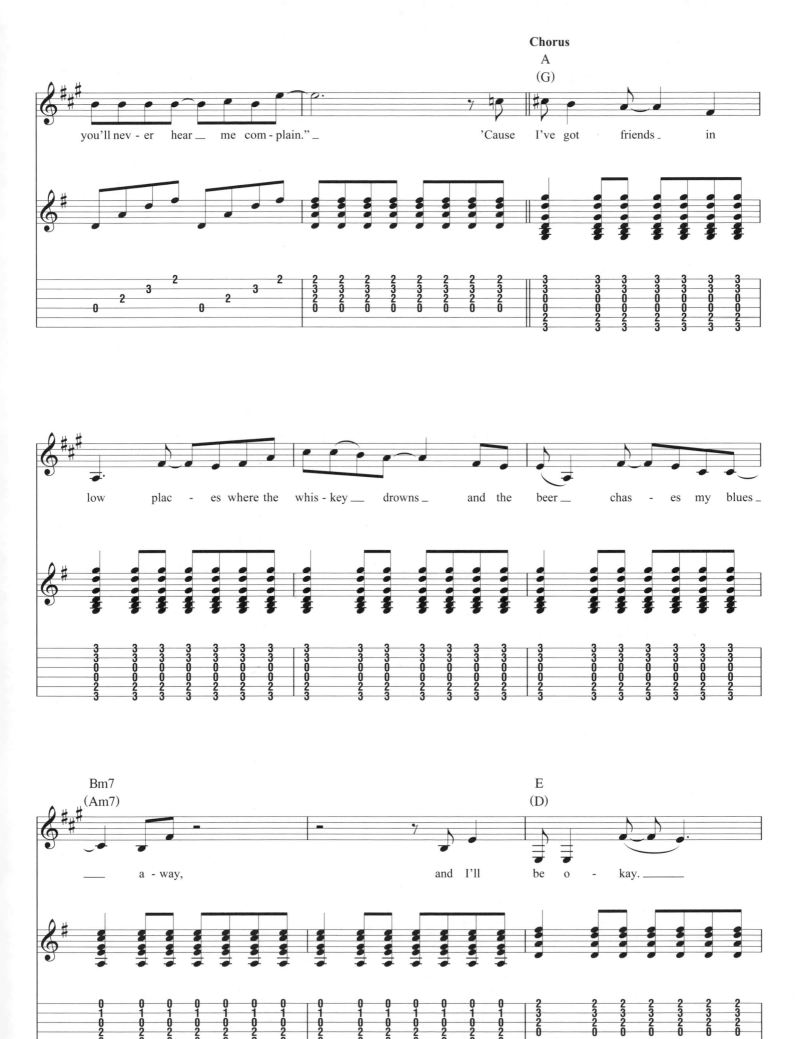

Yeah, I'm not big __ on so - cial gra - ces. Think I'll

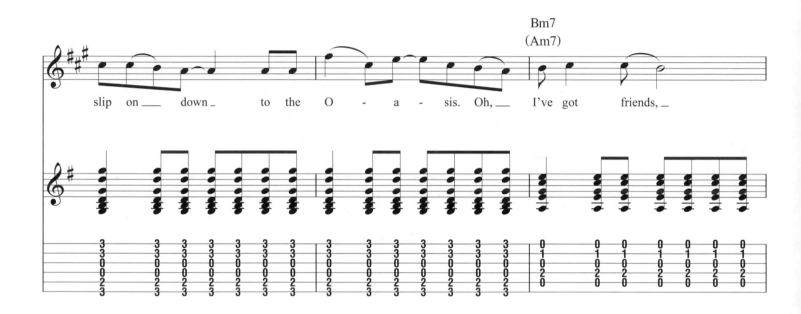

slip on __ down _ to the O - a - sis. Oh, __ I've got friends, _

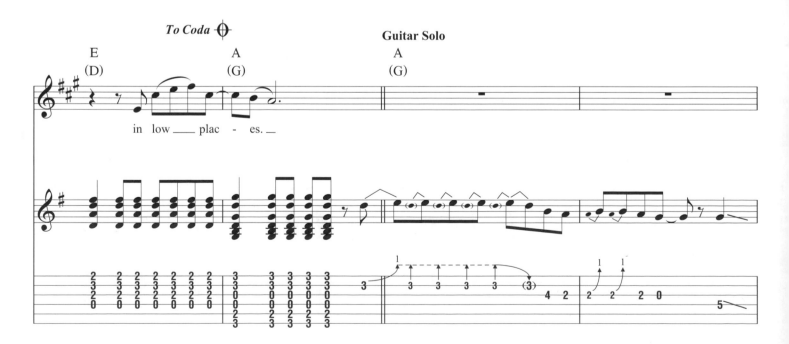

in low __ plac - es. _

D.S. al Coda

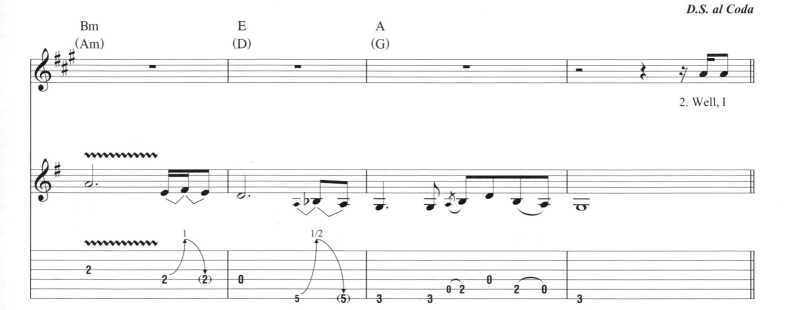

2. Well, I

Coda

Outro-Chorus

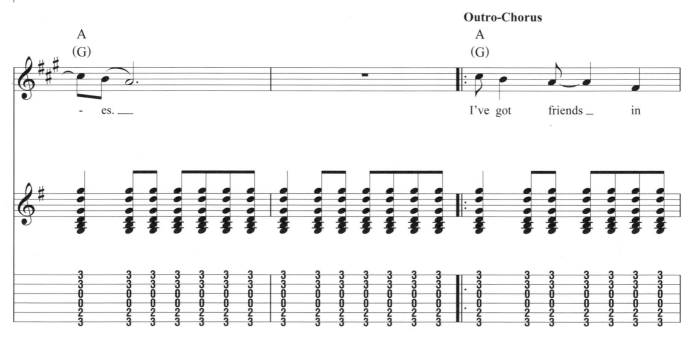

- es. ___

I've got   friends ___   in

low   plac - es where the   whis - key ___ drowns ___   and the   beer ___   chas - es   my   blues ___

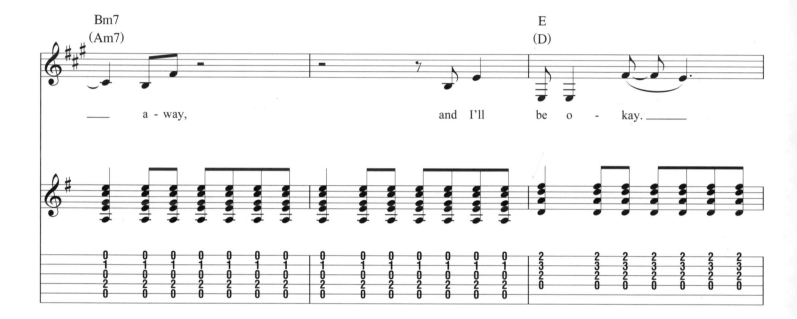

Bm7
(Am7)

E
(D)

___   a - way,   and I'll   be   o - kay. _____

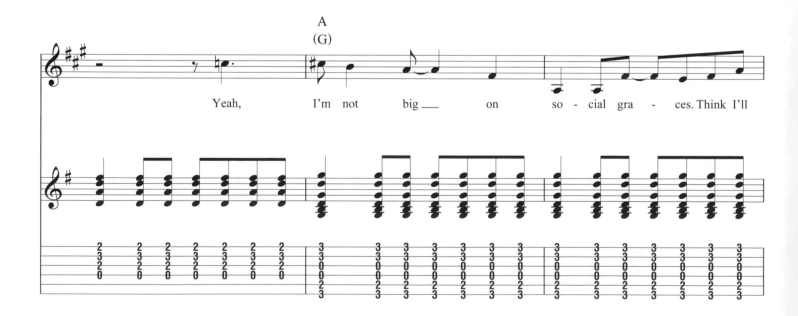

A
(G)

Yeah,   I'm   not   big ___   on   so - cial   gra - ces. Think I'll

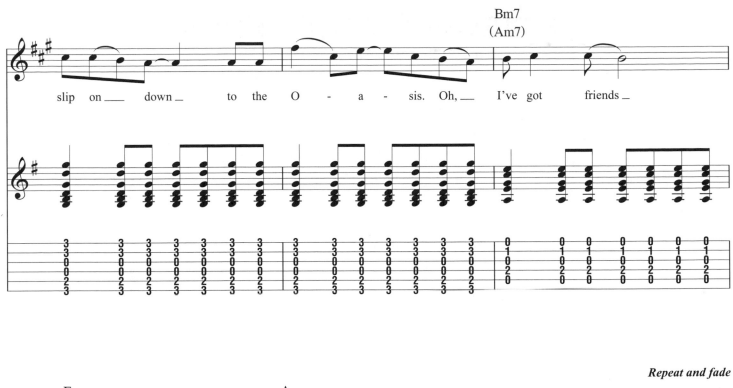

slip on ___ down ___ to the O - a - sis. Oh, ___ I've got friends ___

Repeat and fade

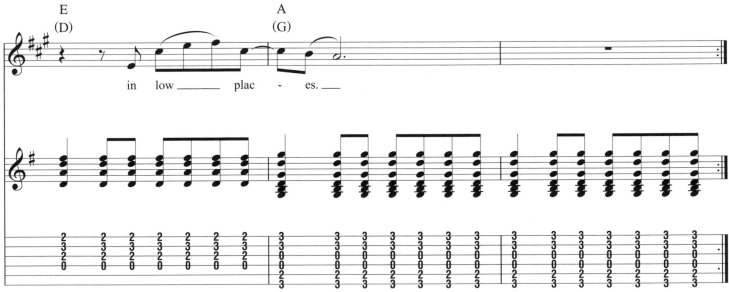

in low _____ plac - es. ___

Additional Lyrics

2. Well, I guess I was wrong, I just don't belong,
   But then, I've been there before.
   Ev'rything's alright, I'll just say goodnight,
   And I'll show myself to the door.
   Hey, I didn't mean to cause a big scene,
   Just give me an hour and then,
   Well, I'll be as high as that ivory tower that you're livin' in.

Folsom Prison Blues

Words and Music by John R. Cash

*Symbols in parentheses represent chord names respective to capoed guitar.
Symbols above reflect actual sounding chords. Capoed fret is "0" in tab.

1. I hear the train a com - in', it's roll - in' 'round the bend.
2., 3., 4. *See additional lyrics*

— And I ain't seen the sun - shine since, I don't know

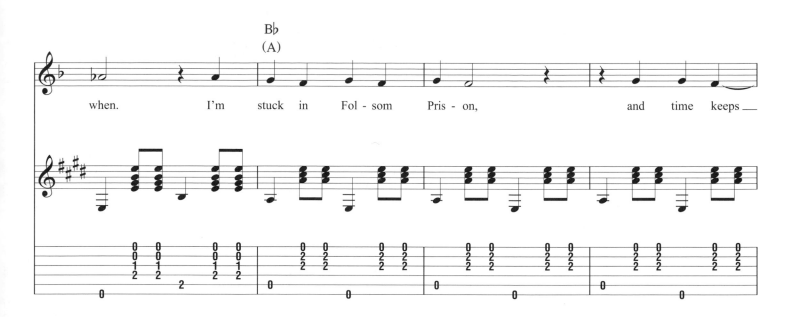

when. I'm stuck in Fol - som Pris - on, and time keeps

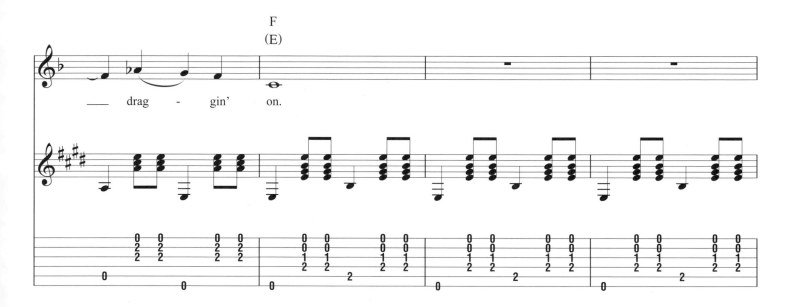

— drag - gin' on.

But that train keeps a roll - in', on down to

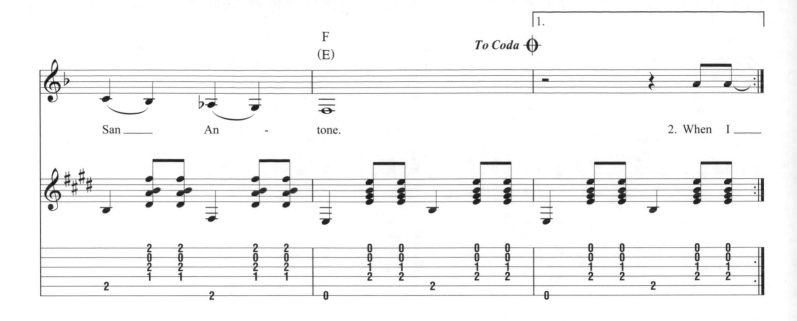

San ____ An - tone.

1.

To Coda

2. When I ____

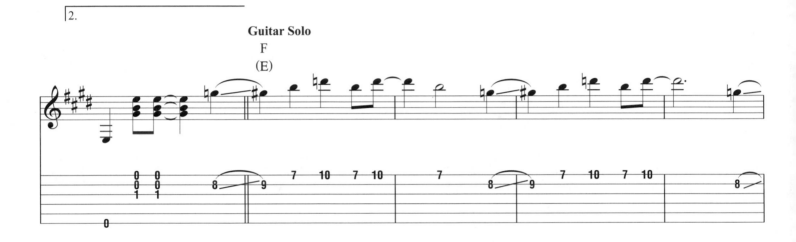

2.

Guitar Solo

F
(E)

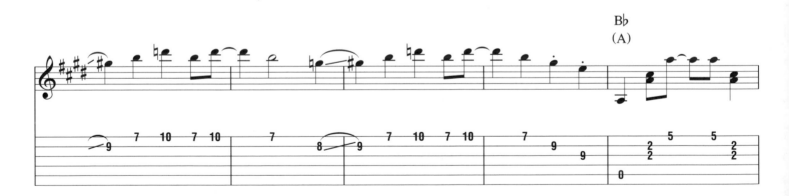

B♭
(A)

F
(E)

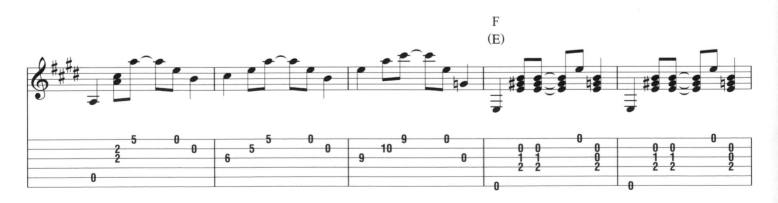

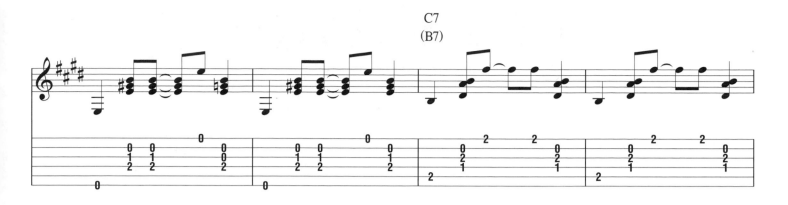

1st time, D.S.
(take 2nd ending)
2nd time, D.S. al Coda

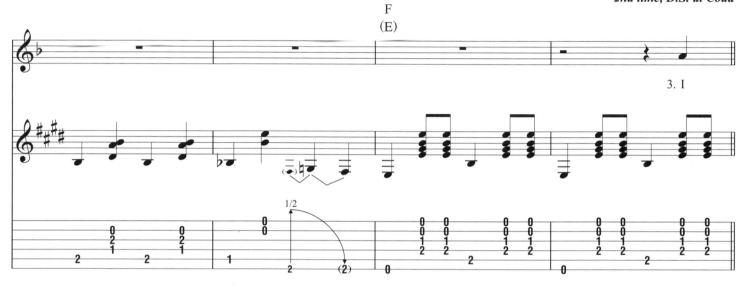

✛ **Coda**

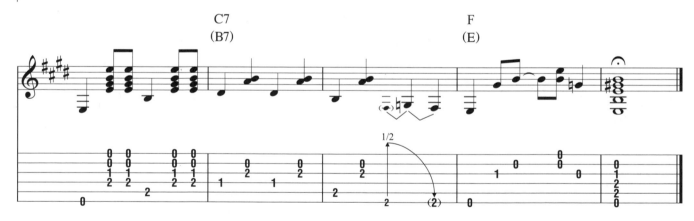

Additional Lyrics

2. When I was just a baby, my mama told me son,
   Always be a good boy; don't ever play with guns.
   But I shot a man in Reno just to watch him die.
   When I hear that whistle blowin' I hang my head and cry.

3. I bet there's rich folk eatin' in a fancy dining car.
   They're prob'ly drinkin' coffee and smokin' big cigars.
   But I know I had it comin', I know I can't be free.
   But those people keep a movin', and that's what tortures me.

4. Well, if they freed me from this prison, if that railroad train was mine,
   I bet I'd move it on a little farther down the line,
   Far from Folsom Prison, that's where I want to stay.
   And I'd let that lonesome whistle blow my blues away.

Tennessee Whiskey

Words and Music by Dean Dillon and Linda Hargrove

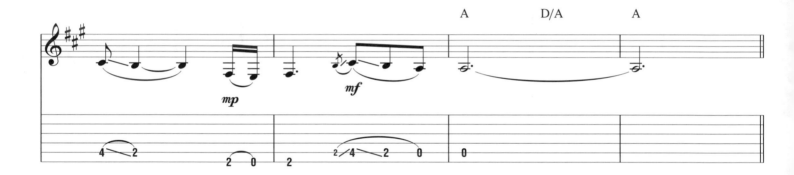

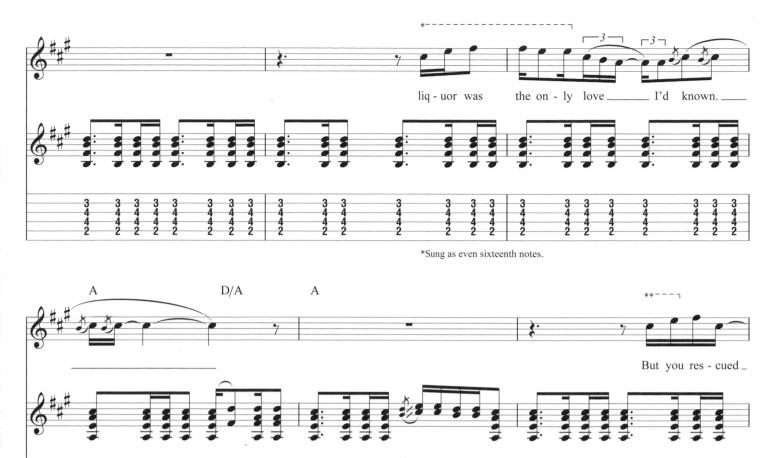

liq-uor was the on-ly love _____ I'd known. _____

*Sung as even sixteenth notes.

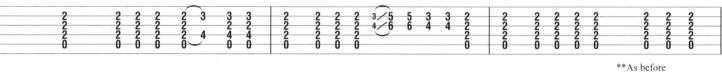

A   D/A   A   **

But you res-cued _

**As before

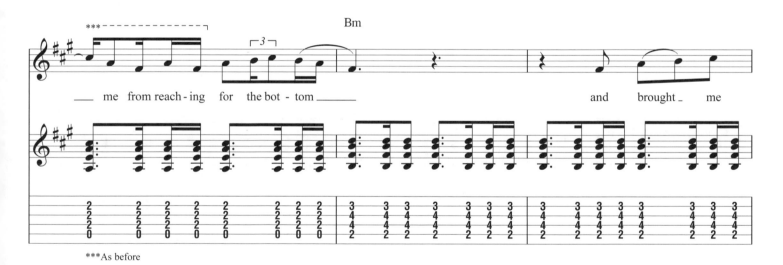

*** Bm

_____ me from reach-ing for the bot - tom _____   and brought _ me

***As before

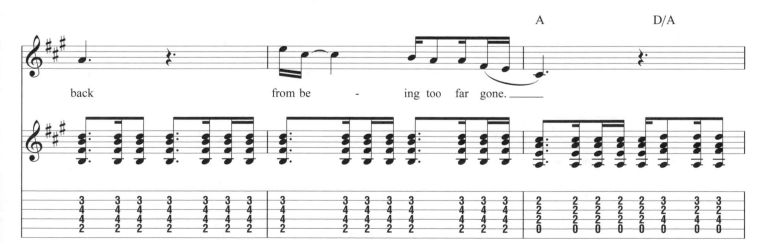

A   D/A

back   from be - ing too far gone. _____

§ **Chorus**

You're _ as smooth as Ten-nes-see whis - key. _

*As before

You're _ as sweet _

**As before

_ as straw - ber-ry wine. _ You're as warm _

***As before

_ as a glass _ of bran - dy. _

†As before

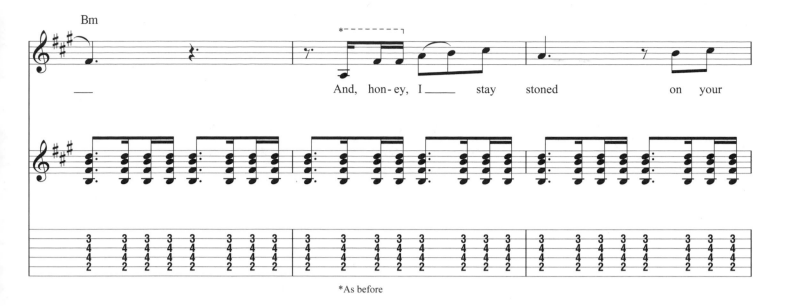

*As before

To Coda 1
To Coda 2

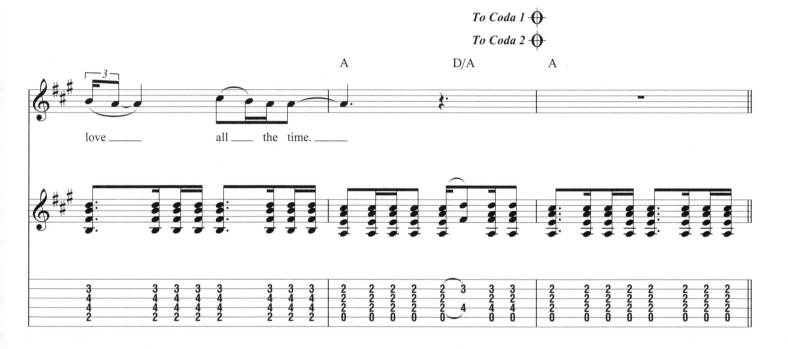

love _____ all _____ the time. _____

Verse

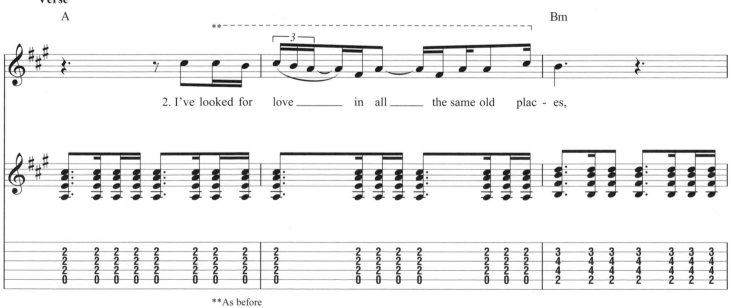

2. I've looked for love _____ in all _____ the same old plac - es,

**As before

*As before

A   D/A   A

**As before

Bm

***As before

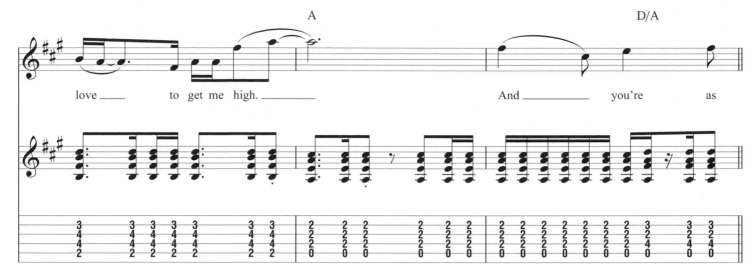

love ____ to get me high. ____ And ____ you're as

Coda 1

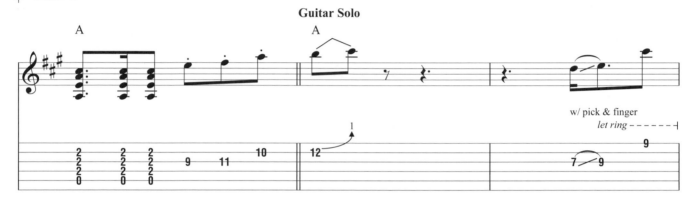

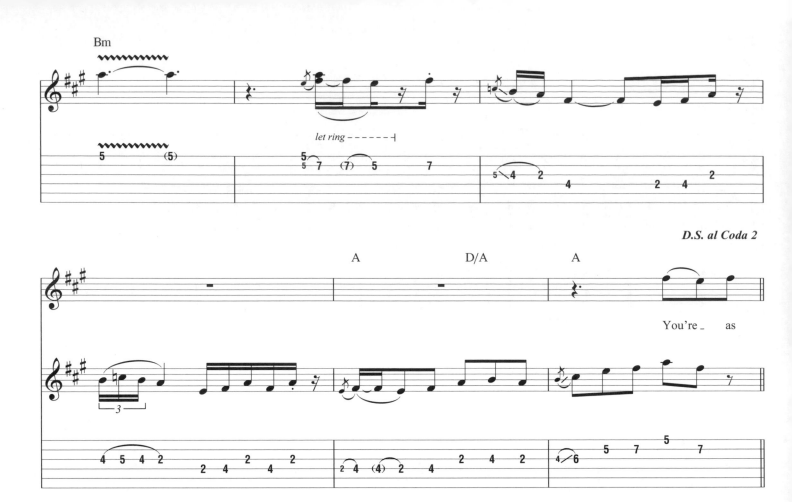

D.S. al Coda 2

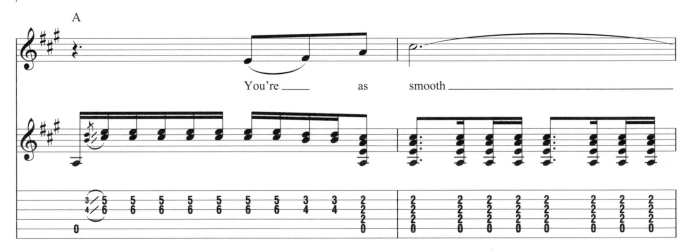

⊕ Coda 2

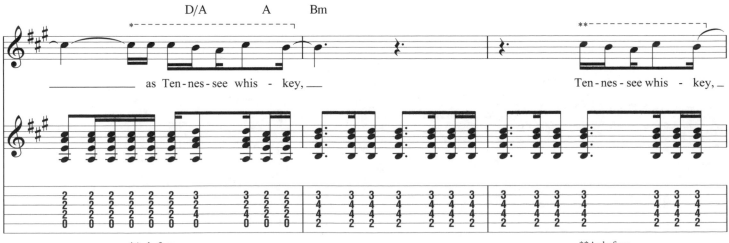

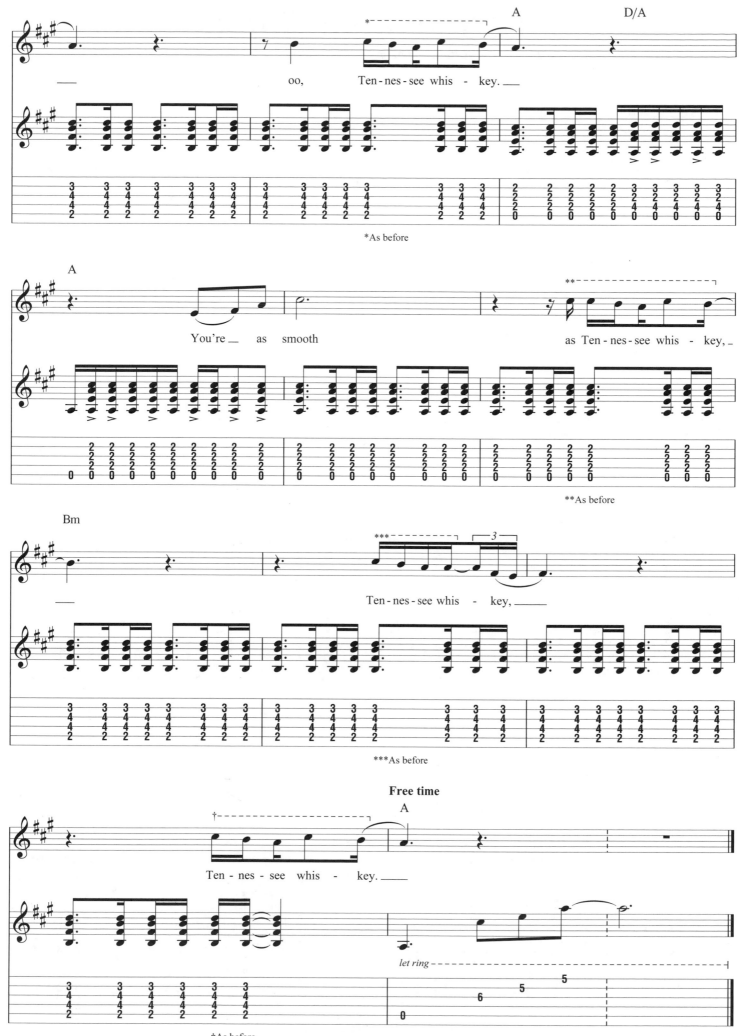

Workin' Man Blues

Words and Music by Merle Haggard

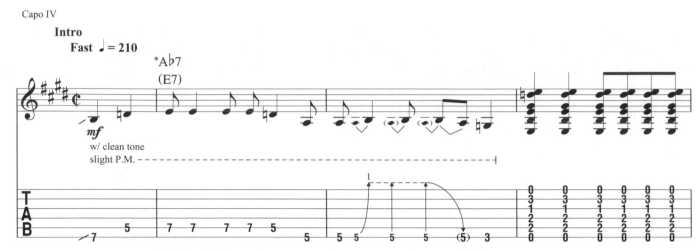

*Chord symbols in parentheses represent chord names respective to capoed guitar.
Symbols above reflect actual sounding chords. Capoed fret is "0" in tab.

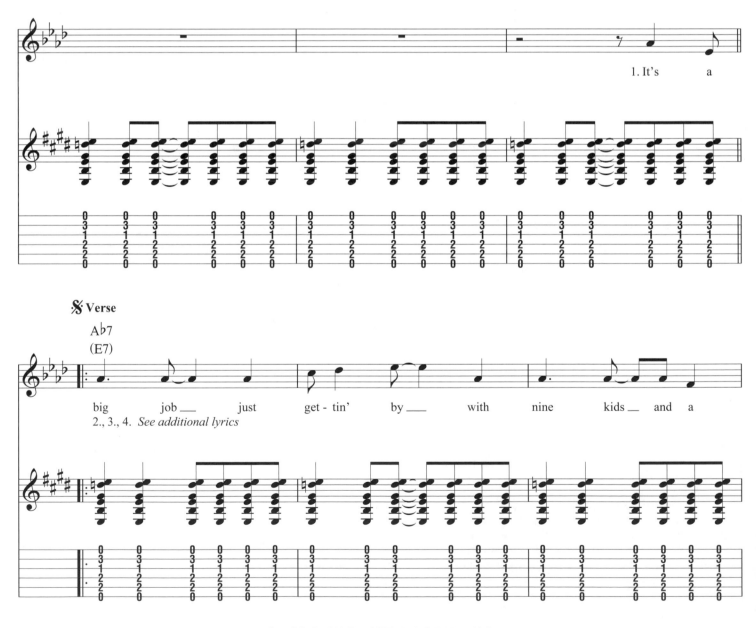

big   job____   just   get-tin'   by____   with   nine   kids____   and   a

2., 3., 4. *See additional lyrics*

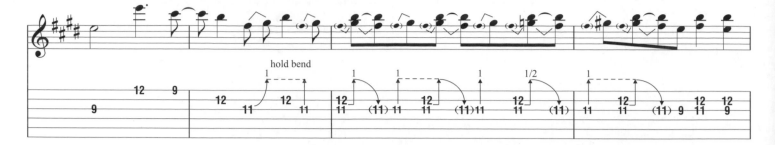

Db7
(A7)

*let ring

*next 10 meas.

Ab7
(E7)

Eb7
(B7)

Db7
(A7)

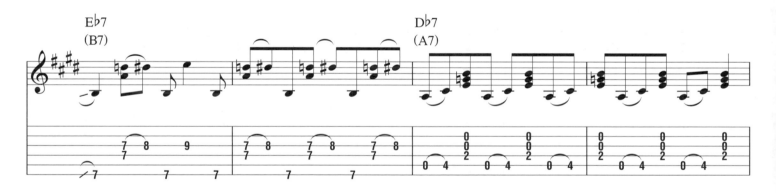

D.S. al Coda

Ab7
(E7)

4. Well,

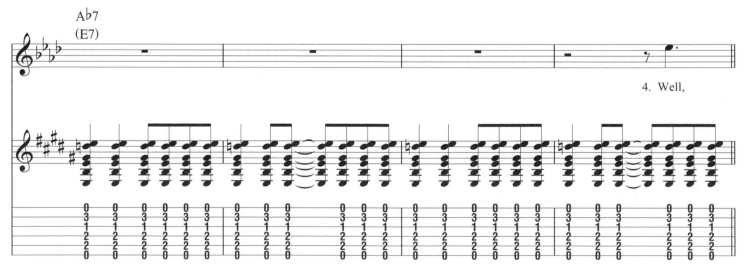

Additional Lyrics

2. I keep my nose to the grind stone,
   Work hard ev'ry day.
   I might get a little tight on the weekend,
   After I draw my pay, then I'll go back workin',
   Come Monday mornin' I'm right back with the crew.
   I'll drink a little beer that evenin',
   Sing a little bit of these workin' man blues.

3. Sometimes I think about leavin', do a little bummin' around.
   I wanna throw my bills out the window, catch a train to another town.
   I go back workin'. Gotta buy my kids a new pair of shoes.
   I drink a little beer in a tavern, cry a little bit of these workin' man blues.
   Here comes that workin' man!

4. Well, hey, hey, the workin' man, workin' man like me.
   I ain't never been on welfare, and that's one place I won't be.
   I'll be workin', long as my two hands are fit to use.
   I'll drink my beer in a tavern, sing a little bit of these workin' man blues.
   This song's for the workin' man!

Wagon Wheel

Words and Music by Bob Dylan and Ketch Secor

Intro
Moderately fast ♩ = 148

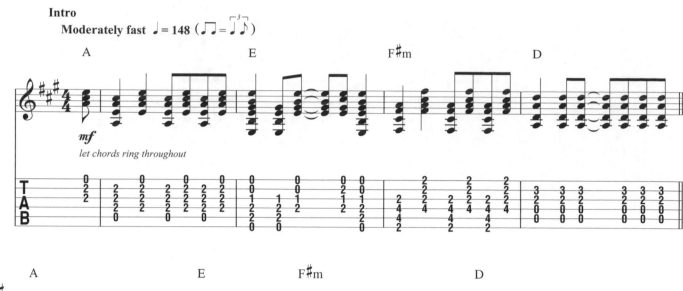

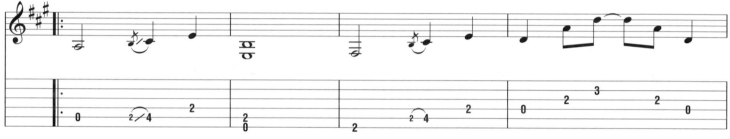

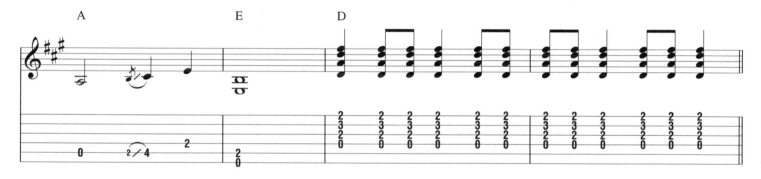

Verse

1. Head- in' down _ south _ to the land _ of the pines, _ I'm thumb- in' my _ way _ in - to North _
2. *See additional lyrics*

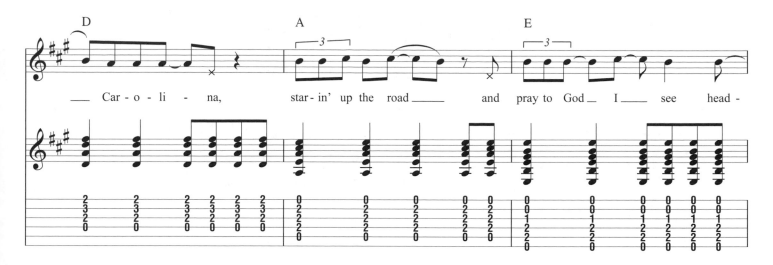

_____ Car - o - li - na, star - in' up the road _____ and pray to God I _____ see head -

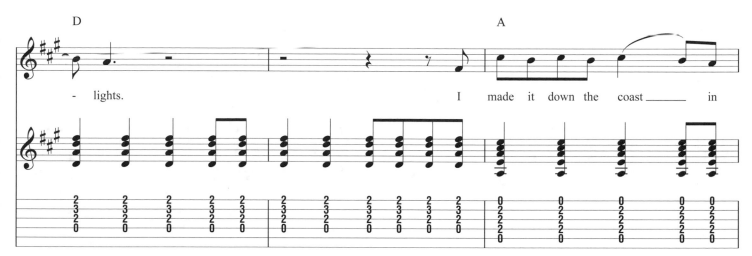

- lights. I made it down the coast _____ in

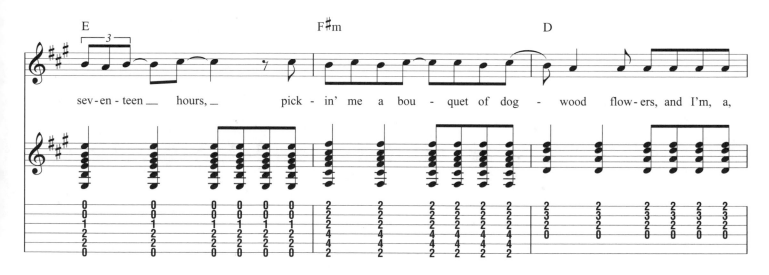

sev - en - teen _____ hours, _____ pick - in' me a bou - quet of dog - wood flow - ers, and I'm, a,

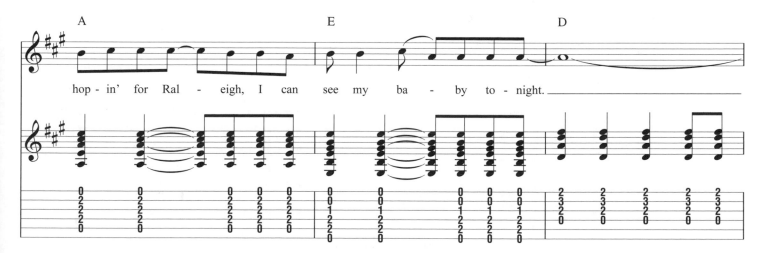

hop - in' for Ral - eigh, I can see my ba - by to - night. _____

Chorus

So, rock ___ me, ma - ma, like a wag - on wheel. ___ Rock ___

___ me, ma - ma, an - y way ___ you feel. ___ Hey, _____

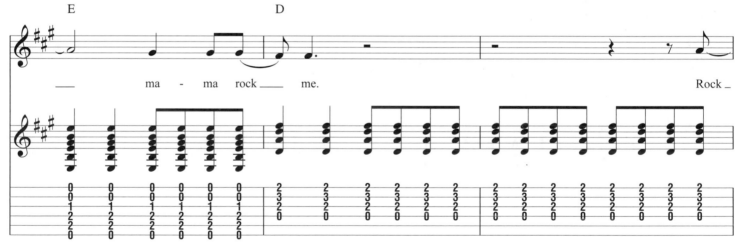

___ ma - ma rock ___ me. Rock ___

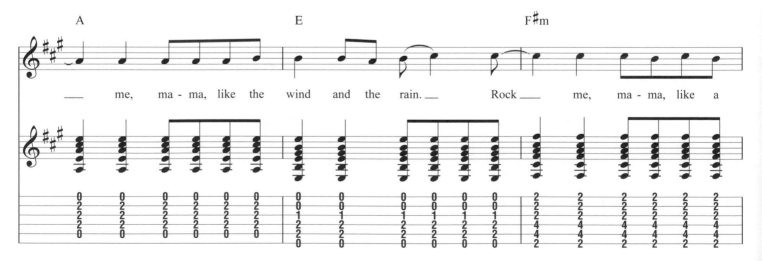

___ me, ma - ma, like the wind and the rain. ___ Rock ___ me, ma - ma, like a

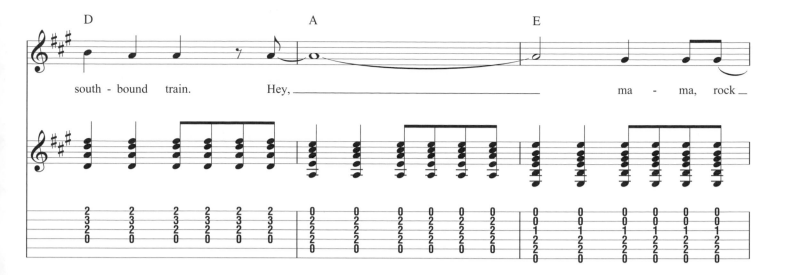

south - bound train.   Hey, _____ ma - ma, rock _

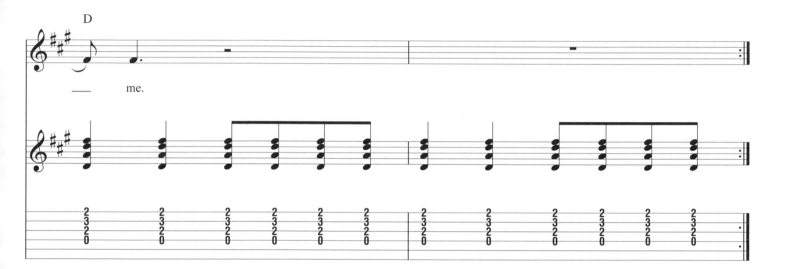

_ me.

Fiddle Solo

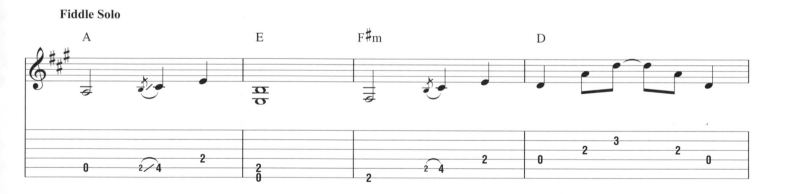

Guitar Solo

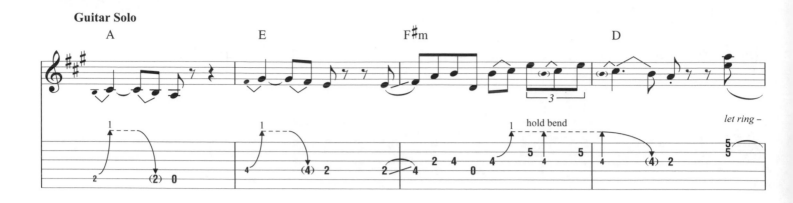

Verse

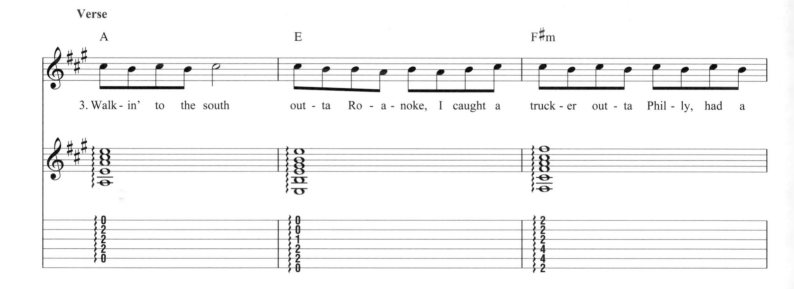

3. Walk-in' to the south out-ta Ro-a-noke, I caught a truck-er out-ta Phil-ly, had a

nice long toke. But he's, a, head-in' west from the Cum-ber-land Gap to

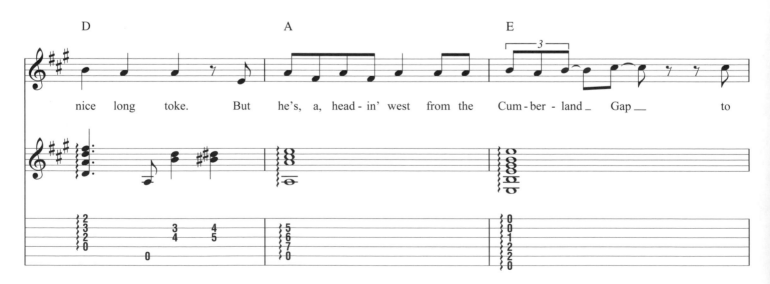

me, ma - ma, an - y way you feel. ___ Hey, ___ ma - ma, rock ___

___ me. ___ Oh, rock ___ me, ma - ma, like the

wind and the rain. ___ Rock ___ me, ma - ma, like a south - bound train.

End half-time feel

Hey, ___ ma - ma, rock ___ me. Oh, ___ rock

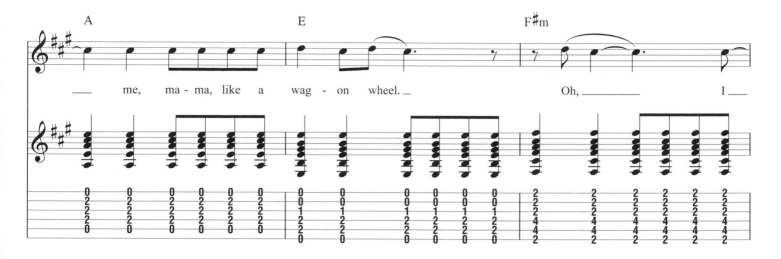

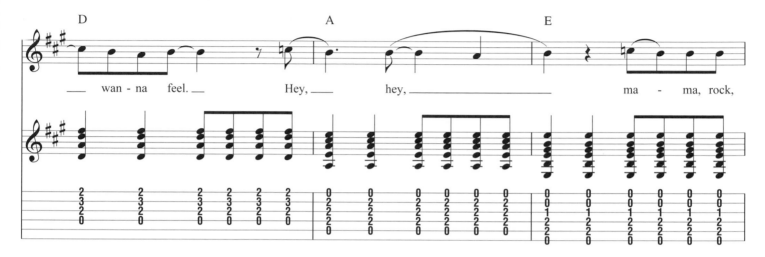

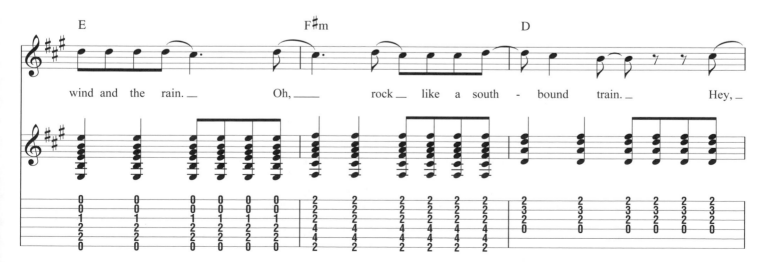

yeah, ___ yeah, ___ a, ma - ma, rock, you will rock ___ me. Rock ___

Outro

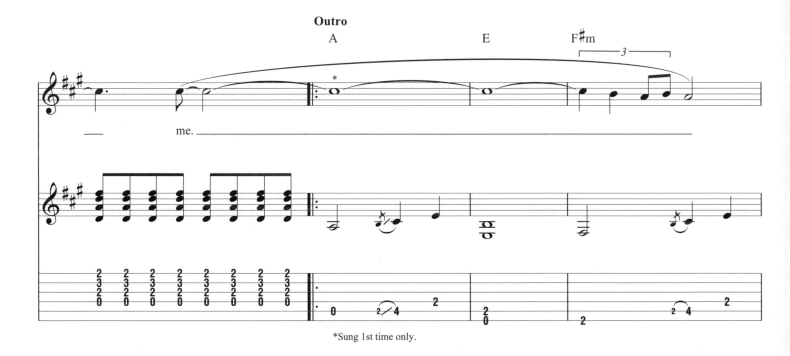

___ me. _____

*Sung 1st time only.

Repeat and fade

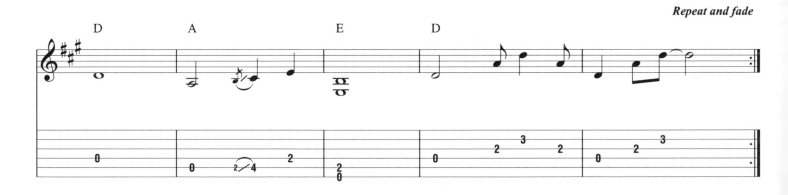

Additional Lyrics

2. I'm runnin' from the cold up in New England,
   I was born to be a fiddler in an old-time string band.
   My baby plays the guitar; I pick a banjo now.
   Oh, north country winters keep, a, gettin' me down.
   Lost my money playin' poker so I had to leave town.
   But I ain't, a, turnin' back to livin' that old life no more.

GUITAR NOTATION LEGEND

THE MUSICAL STAFF shows pitches and rhythms and is divided by bar lines into measures. Pitches are named after the first seven letters of the alphabet.

TABLATURE graphically represents the guitar fingerboard. Each horizontal line represents a string, and each number represents a fret.

4th string, 2nd fret   1st & 2nd strings open, played together   open D chord

HALF-STEP BEND: Strike the note and bend up 1/2 step.

WHOLE-STEP BEND: Strike the note and bend up one step.

GRACE NOTE BEND: Strike the note and immediately bend up as indicated.

SLIGHT (MICROTONE) BEND: Strike the note and bend up 1/4 step.

BEND AND RELEASE: Strike the note and bend up as indicated, then release back to the original note. Only the first note is struck.

PRE-BEND: Bend the note as indicated, then strike it.

VIBRATO: The string is vibrated by rapidly bending and releasing the note with the fretting hand.

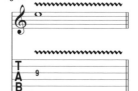

PALM MUTING: The note is partially muted by the pick hand lightly touching the string(s) just before the bridge.

HAMMER-ON: Strike the first (lower) note with one finger, then sound the higher note (on the same string) with another finger by fretting it without picking.

PULL-OFF: Place both fingers on the notes to be sounded. Strike the first note and without picking, pull the finger off to sound the second (lower) note.

LEGATO SLIDE: Strike the first note and then slide the same fret-hand finger up or down to the second note. The second note is not struck.

SHIFT SLIDE: Same as legato slide, except the second note is struck.

TRILL: Very rapidly alternate between the notes indicated by continuously hammering on and pulling off.

TAPPING: Hammer ("tap") the fret indicated with the pick-hand index or middle finger and pull off to the note fretted by the fret hand.

NATURAL HARMONIC: Strike the note while the fret-hand lightly touches the string directly over the fret indicated.

PINCH HARMONIC: The note is fretted normally and a harmonic is produced by adding the edge of the thumb or the tip of the index finger of the pick hand to the normal pick attack.

TREMOLO PICKING: The note is picked as rapidly and continuously as possible.

VIBRATO BAR DIVE AND RETURN: The pitch of the note or chord is dropped a specified number of steps (in rhythm), then returned to the original pitch.

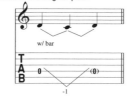

VIBRATO BAR SCOOP: Depress the bar just before striking the note, then quickly release the bar.

VIBRATO BAR DIP: Strike the note and then immediately drop a specified number of steps, then release back to the original pitch.

Additional Musical Definitions

(accent)	• Accentuate note (play it louder).
(staccato)	• Play the note short.
D.S. al Coda	• Go back to the sign (%), then play until the measure marked "**To Coda**," then skip to the section labelled "**Coda**."
D.C. al Fine	• Go back to the beginning of the song and play until the measure marked "**Fine**" (end).

Fill • Label used to identify a brief melodic figure which is to be inserted into the arrangement.

N.C. • Harmony is implied.

• Repeat measures between signs.

• When a repeated section has different endings, play the first ending only the first time and the second ending only the second time.

HAL•LEONARD GUITAR PLAY-ALONG

This series will help you play your favorite songs quickly and easily. Just follow **INCLUDES TAB** the tab and listen to the audio to the hear how the guitar should sound, and then play along using the separate backing tracks. Audio files also include software to slow down the tempo without changing pitch. The melody and lyrics are included in the book so that you can sing or simply follow along.

Complete song lists available online.

VOL. 1 – ROCK	00699570 / $16.99
VOL. 2 – ACOUSTIC	00699569 / $16.99
VOL. 3 – HARD ROCK	00699573 / $17.99
VOL. 4 – POP/ROCK	00699571 / $16.99
VOL. 5 – THREE CHORD SONGS	00300985 / $16.99
VOL. 6 – '90S ROCK	00298615 / $16.99
VOL. 7 – BLUES	00699575 / $17.99
VOL. 8 – ROCK	00699585 / $16.99
VOL. 9 – EASY ACOUSTIC SONGS	00151708 / $16.99
VOL. 10 – ACOUSTIC	00699586 / $16.95
VOL. 11 – EARLY ROCK	00699579 / $15.99
VOL. 12 – ROCK POP	00291724 / $16.99
VOL. 14 – BLUES ROCK	00699582 / $16.99
VOL. 15 – R&B	00699583 / $17.99
VOL. 16 – JAZZ	00699584 / $15.95
VOL. 17 – COUNTRY	00699588 / $16.99
VOL. 18 – ACOUSTIC ROCK	00699577 / $15.95
VOL. 20 – ROCKABILLY	00699580 / $16.99
VOL. 21 – SANTANA	00174525 / $17.99
VOL. 22 – CHRISTMAS	00699600 / $15.99
VOL. 23 – SURF	00699635 / $16.99
VOL. 24 – ERIC CLAPTON	00699649 / $17.99
VOL. 25 – THE BEATLES	00198265 / $17.99
VOL. 26 – ELVIS PRESLEY	00699643 / $16.99
VOL. 27 – DAVID LEE ROTH	00699645 / $16.95
VOL. 28 – GREG KOCH	00699646 / $17.99
VOL. 29 – BOB SEGER	00699647 / $16.99
VOL. 30 – KISS	00699644 / $16.99
VOL. 32 – THE OFFSPRING	00699653 / $14.95
VOL. 33 – ACOUSTIC CLASSICS	00699656 / $17.99
VOL. 34 – CLASSIC ROCK	00699658 / $17.99
VOL. 35 – HAIR METAL	00699660 / $17.99
VOL. 36 – SOUTHERN ROCK	00699661 / $19.99
VOL. 37 – ACOUSTIC UNPLUGGED	00699662 / $22.99
VOL. 38 – BLUES	00699663 / $17.99
VOL. 39 – '80s METAL	00699664 / $16.99
VOL. 40 – INCUBUS	00699668 / $17.95
VOL. 41 – ERIC CLAPTON	00699669 / $17.99
VOL. 42 – COVER BAND HITS	00211597 / $16.99
VOL. 43 – LYNYRD SKYNYRD	00699681 / $19.99
VOL. 44 – JAZZ GREATS	00699689 / $16.99
VOL. 45 – TV THEMES	00699718 / $14.95
VOL. 46 – MAINSTREAM ROCK	00699722 / $16.95
VOL. 47 – JIMI HENDRIX SMASH HITS	00699723 / $19.99
VOL. 48 – AEROSMITH CLASSICS	00699724 / $17.99
VOL. 49 – STEVIE RAY VAUGHAN	00699725 / $17.99
VOL. 50 – VAN HALEN: 1978-1984	00110269 / $19.99
VOL. 51 – ALTERNATIVE '90s	00699727 / $14.99
VOL. 52 – FUNK	00699728 / $15.99
VOL. 53 – DISCO	00699729 / $14.99
VOL. 54 – HEAVY METAL	00699730 / $16.99
VOL. 55 – POP METAL	00699731 / $14.95
VOL. 56 – FOO FIGHTERS	00699749 / $17.99
VOL. 57 – GUNS 'N' ROSES	00159922 / $17.99
VOL. 58 – BLINK 182	00699772 / $14.95
VOL. 59 – CHET ATKINS	00702347 / $17.99
VOL. 60 – 3 DOORS DOWN	00699774 / $14.95
VOL. 62 – CHRISTMAS CAROLS	00699798 / $12.95
VOL. 63 – CREEDENCE CLEARWATER REVIVAL	00699802 / $16.99
VOL. 64 – ULTIMATE OZZY OSBOURNE	00699803 / $17.99
VOL. 66 – THE ROLLING STONES	00699807 / $17.99
VOL. 67 – BLACK SABBATH	00699808 / $16.99
VOL. 68 – PINK FLOYD – DARK SIDE OF THE MOON	00699809 / $16.99
VOL. 71 – CHRISTIAN ROCK	00699824 / $14.95

VOL. 72 – ACOUSTIC '90s	00699827 / $14.95
VOL. 73 – BLUESY ROCK	00699829 / $16.99
VOL. 74 – SIMPLE STRUMMING SONGS	00151706 / $19.99
VOL. 75 – TOM PETTY	00699882 / $17.99
VOL. 76 – COUNTRY HITS	00699884 / $16.99
VOL. 77 – BLUEGRASS	00699910 / $15.99
VOL. 78 – NIRVANA	00700132 / $16.99
VOL. 79 – NEIL YOUNG	00700133 / $24.99
VOL. 80 – ACOUSTIC ANTHOLOGY	00700175 / $19.95
VOL. 81 – ROCK ANTHOLOGY	00700176 / $22.99
VOL. 82 – EASY ROCK SONGS	00700177 / $17.99
VOL. 84 – STEELY DAN	00700200 / $19.99
VOL. 85 – THE POLICE	00700269 / $16.99
VOL. 86 – BOSTON	00700465 / $16.99
VOL. 87 – ACOUSTIC WOMEN	00700763 / $14.99
VOL. 88 – GRUNGE	00700467 / $16.99
VOL. 89 – REGGAE	00700468 / $15.99
VOL. 90 – CLASSICAL POP	00700469 / $14.99
VOL. 91 – BLUES INSTRUMENTALS	00700505 / $17.99
VOL. 92 – EARLY ROCK INSTRUMENTALS	00700506 / $15.99
VOL. 93 – ROCK INSTRUMENTALS	00700507 / $16.99
VOL. 94 – SLOW BLUES	00700508 / $16.99
VOL. 95 – BLUES CLASSICS	00700509 / $15.99
VOL. 96 – BEST COUNTRY HITS	00211615 / $16.99
VOL. 97 – CHRISTMAS CLASSICS	00236542 / $14.99
VOL. 98 – ROCK BAND	00700704 / $14.95
VOL. 99 – ZZ TOP	00700762 / $16.99
VOL. 100 – B.B. KING	00700466 / $16.99
VOL. 101 – SONGS FOR BEGINNERS	00701917 / $14.99
VOL. 102 – CLASSIC PUNK	00700769 / $14.99
VOL. 103 – SWITCHFOOT	00700773 / $16.99
VOL. 104 – DUANE ALLMAN	00700846 / $17.99
VOL. 105 – LATIN	00700939 / $16.99
VOL. 106 – WEEZER	00700958 / $14.99
VOL. 107 – CREAM	00701069 / $16.99
VOL. 108 – THE WHO	00701053 / $16.99
VOL. 109 – STEVE MILLER	00701054 / $19.99
VOL. 110 – SLIDE GUITAR HITS	00701055 / $16.99
VOL. 111 – JOHN MELLENCAMP	00701056 / $14.99
VOL. 112 – QUEEN	00701052 / $16.99
VOL. 113 – JIM CROCE	00701058 / $17.99
VOL. 114 – BON JOVI	00701060 / $16.99
VOL. 115 – JOHNNY CASH	00701070 / $16.99
VOL. 116 – THE VENTURES	00701124 / $16.99
VOL. 117 – BRAD PAISLEY	00701224 / $16.99
VOL. 118 – ERIC JOHNSON	00701353 / $16.99
VOL. 119 – AC/DC CLASSICS	00701356 / $17.99
VOL. 120 – PROGRESSIVE ROCK	00701457 / $14.99
VOL. 121 – U2	00701508 / $16.99
VOL. 122 – CROSBY, STILLS & NASH	00701610 / $16.99
VOL. 123 – LENNON & McCARTNEY ACOUSTIC	00701614 / $16.99
VOL. 124 – SMOOTH JAZZ	00200664 / $16.99
VOL. 125 – JEFF BECK	00701687 / $17.99
VOL. 126 – BOB MARLEY	00701701 / $16.99
VOL. 127 – 1970s ROCK	00701739 / $16.99
VOL. 128 – 1960s ROCK	00701740 / $14.99
VOL. 129 – MEGADETH	00701741 / $17.99
VOL. 130 – IRON MAIDEN	00701742 / $17.99
VOL. 131 – 1990s ROCK	00701743 / $14.99
VOL. 132 – COUNTRY ROCK	00701757 / $15.99
VOL. 133 – TAYLOR SWIFT	00701894 / $16.99
VOL. 134 – AVENGED SEVENFOLD	00701906 / $16.99
VOL. 135 – MINOR BLUES	00151350 / $17.99
VOL. 136 – GUITAR THEMES	00701922 / $14.99
VOL. 137 – IRISH TUNES	00701966 / $15.99
VOL. 138 – BLUEGRASS CLASSICS	00701967 / $17.99

VOL. 139 – GARY MOORE	00702370 / $16.99
VOL. 140 – MORE STEVIE RAY VAUGHAN	00702396 / $17.99
VOL. 141 – ACOUSTIC HITS	00702401 / $16.99
VOL. 142 – GEORGE HARRISON	00237697 / $17.99
VOL. 143 – SLASH	00702425 / $19.99
VOL. 144 – DJANGO REINHARDT	00702531 / $16.99
VOL. 145 – DEF LEPPARD	00702532 / $17.99
VOL. 146 – ROBERT JOHNSON	00702533 / $16.99
VOL. 147 – SIMON & GARFUNKEL	14041591 / $16.99
VOL. 148 – BOB DYLAN	14041592 / $16.99
VOL. 149 – AC/DC HITS	14041593 / $17.99
VOL. 150 – ZAKK WYLDE	02501717 / $16.99
VOL. 151 – J.S. BACH	02501730 / $16.99
VOL. 152 – JOE BONAMASSA	02501751 / $19.99
VOL. 153 – RED HOT CHILI PEPPERS	00702990 / $19.99
VOL. 154 – GLEE	00703018 / $16.99
VOL. 155 – ERIC CLAPTON UNPLUGGED	00703085 / $16.99
VOL. 156 – SLAYER	00703770 / $19.99
VOL. 157 – FLEETWOOD MAC	00101382 / $17.99
VOL. 159 – WES MONTGOMERY	00102593 / $19.99
VOL. 160 – T-BONE WALKER	00102641 / $17.99
VOL. 161 – THE EAGLES ACOUSTIC	00102659 / $17.99
VOL. 162 – THE EAGLES HITS	00102667 / $17.99
VOL. 163 – PANTERA	00103036 / $17.99
VOL. 164 – VAN HALEN: 1986-1995	00110270 / $17.99
VOL. 165 – GREEN DAY	00210343 / $17.99
VOL. 166 – MODERN BLUES	00700764 / $16.99
VOL. 167 – DREAM THEATER	00111938 / $24.99
VOL. 168 – KISS	00113421 / $17.99
VOL. 169 – TAYLOR SWIFT	00115982 / $16.99
VOL. 170 – THREE DAYS GRACE	00117337 / $16.99
VOL. 171 – JAMES BROWN	00117420 / $16.99
VOL. 172 – THE DOOBIE BROTHERS	00119670 / $16.99
VOL. 173 – TRANS-SIBERIAN ORCHESTRA	00119907 / $19.99
VOL. 174 – SCORPIONS	00122119 / $16.99
VOL. 175 – MICHAEL SCHENKER	00122127 / $17.99
VOL. 176 – BLUES BREAKERS WITH JOHN MAYALL & ERIC CLAPTON	00122132 / $19.99
VOL. 177 – ALBERT KING	00123271 / $16.99
VOL. 178 – JASON MRAZ	00124165 / $17.99
VOL. 179 – RAMONES	00127073 / $16.99
VOL. 180 – BRUNO MARS	00129706 / $16.99
VOL. 181 – JACK JOHNSON	00129854 / $16.99
VOL. 182 – SOUNDGARDEN	00138161 / $17.99
VOL. 183 – BUDDY GUY	00138240 / $17.99
VOL. 184 – KENNY WAYNE SHEPHERD	00138258 / $17.99
VOL. 185 – JOE SATRIANI	00139457 / $17.99
VOL. 186 – GRATEFUL DEAD	00139459 / $17.99
VOL. 187 – JOHN DENVER	00140839 / $17.99
VOL. 188 – MÖTLEY CRÜE	00141145 / $17.99
VOL. 189 – JOHN MAYER	00144350 / $17.99
VOL. 190 – DEEP PURPLE	00146152 / $17.99
VOL. 191 – PINK FLOYD CLASSICS	00146164 / $17.99
VOL. 192 – JUDAS PRIEST	00151352 / $17.99
VOL. 193 – STEVE VAI	00156028 / $19.99
VOL. 194 – PEARL JAM	00157925 / $17.99
VOL. 195 – METALLICA: 1983-1988	00234291 / $19.99
VOL. 196 – METALLICA: 1991-2016	00234292 / $19.99

Prices, contents, and availability subject to change without notice.

HAL•LEONARD

www.halleonard.com

082

17